# War Psalms
## of the
## Prince of Peace

# War Psalms
# of the
# Prince of Peace

## Lessons From the Imprecatory Psalms

James E. Adams

*Presbyterian and Reformed Publishing Company*
*Phillipsburg, New Jersey*

Unless otherwise noted, all Scripture quotations are from the HOLY BIBLE, NEW INTERNATIONAL VERSION. Copyright © 1973, 1978, 1984 International Bible Society. Used by permission of Zondervan Bible Publishers.


Manufactured in the United States of America.

**Library of Congress Cataloging-in-Publication Data**

Adams, James E., 1946–
    War psalms of the Prince of Peace : lessons from the imprecatory
psalms / James E. Adams.
        p.        cm.
    Includes bibliographical references and index.
    ISBN 0-87552-093-6
    1. Bible. O.T. Psalms–Criticism, interpretation, etc.
    2. Blessing and cursing in the Bible. I. Title. II. Title:
    Imprecatory psalms.
    BS1445.I46A32   1991
    223'.206–dc20                                                91-13140

99   98   97   96   95   94   93   92        7   6   5   4   3   2

To my wife,

**Nancy Anne Radu de Adams,**

*"bone of my bones and flesh of my flesh,"*
*whose participation in the composition*
*of this volume makes it* our *book.*

# Contents

# Foreword

I cannot enthusiastically enough commend Jim Adams (no relative of mine except in the Second Adam) for the work he has done in dealing with a difficult and all-too-often neglected area of preaching! And, of even greater importance, he has done so sympathetically and biblically.

Pastor, how often have you shied away from preaching on these large tracts of scriptural turf called the "imprecatory psalms"? How often have you wondered how they could be a part of the Word of God? Well, you have to wonder no longer; you need avoid them no more—*War Psalms of the Prince of Peace* will both explain their purpose and teach you how to proclaim God's truth from them.

As I write, we have been three days at war with Iraq. When this book comes into your hands, that war will (God grant) be over. But, put yourself back into that period as you read. And, remember, in these psalms it is God who is at war with His enemies.

This book has been needed for quite a long time. At last you have the privilege of reading it. While it is not always pleasant reading—because of the human wickedness and rebellion that occasioned these psalms—you will find Dr. Adams's work both instructive and invaluable.

Jay E. Adams
Enoree, South Carolina, 1991

# Preface

My special interest in the Psalms was sparked by Dr. Martyn
Lloyd-Jones in the summer of 1969. In his last message at a pastor's conference in Carlisle, Pennsylvania, Dr. Lloyd-Jones,
preaching with resonant voice and relevant insight, said to us:

> Look at the psalmist. Look at some of those imprecatory psalms.
> What are they? There is nothing wrong with them. It's just the
> zeal of the psalmist. He's grieved and troubled because these
> people are not honoring God as they should be. That's his su-
> preme concern.

Dr. Lloyd-Jones's words prompted me to look at the imprecatory psalms again. As I read them, I was awed by these dramatic
prayers for the annihilation of enemies. I gained a deeper appreciation for the Psalms in general, but I remained at a loss about
how certain psalms should be prayed and preached. I knew that
all of our preaching and teaching of God's Word must come from
the context of God's great love and the forgiveness we find in
Jesus Christ. But how was I to pray and preach psalms of vengeance?

In the summer of 1983 I chose the imprecatory psalms as my
area of specialization for the Doctor of Ministry program at Westminster Seminary in California, and so began my formal study of
them. I found that many theological disputes spring from the
Psalms. One of the most important of them concerns who is
speaking the psalms of imprecation. The title and historical setting of various psalms help determine the human author, but are
these *merely* human words? This is a crucial issue. On the one

hand, if Christ is the speaker, how can the "guilty" (penitential) psalms be understood? On the other hand, if David alone is the speaker, what do we do with the "self-righteous" words of the Psalms? Scholars have wrestled with these problems for centuries.

On a more personal level, the most penetrating question I needed to answer for myself and others was, What is my relationship as a Christian to the Psalms today? We need more than a passive understanding to satisfy our minds: we need instruction for *living!*

Christians everywhere read the Psalms with much enjoyment and personal blessing. But as the Psalms are studied and considered in more detail, perplexing questions inevitably arise. Many people in the congregations where I've pastored have expressed misgivings and bewilderment over the curses found in the Psalms. One of the purposes of this book is to provide a biblical response to such concerns.

I began my studies of the imprecatory psalms by reading them through many times, trying to determine their intrinsic significance as first written by the psalmist under divine inspiration. I studied these cries for justice in the original Hebrew text, as well as in some fifteen different translations. I read hundreds of commentaries and every article I could find, and as you can imagine, I exposed myself to many differing points of view!

I thank God that we have a great heritage of Christ-exalting literature on the Psalms. Unfortunately, many people have dismissed this literature *en toto* because it contains occasional fanciful interpretations or exegetical quirks. Both Augustine and Luther have quirks and fanciful thoughts at times, but the one who dismisses their contributions deprives himself of great riches. Part of the wealth of Spurgeon's *Treasury of David* is the "Quaint Sayings" he mined and compiled from previous literature on the Psalms. Of more modern literature I have quoted several segments from the writings of Dietrich Bonhoeffer, although I stand opposed to the theological camp with which he is often identified. To have ignored his profound insights would, I believe, have been an unjustifiable loss to writer and readers alike.

Before putting into print the answers that I believe Scripture gives us to the puzzling prayers of the Psalms, I first taught these principles and applications in a theological seminary several years ago. In addition, I have given seminars on the imprecatory psalms in the United States and parts of Latin America. Some of the pastors I've had the privilege of instructing in these seminars have become so excited with these truths that they've begun to preach Christ from the Psalms for the first time. Many have requested that this book be published not just in English, but in Spanish as well. One dear Colombian pastor was astonished to see how these psalms address the social needs of the suffering people of God in his country. He said, "Latin America needs to learn how to cry to God for justice and vindication in the name of Christ. No one has ever taught us to understand and preach Christ from these psalms!"

To my knowledge, this is the first book of its kind in the English language. I hope it will be the first of many, since there is so much more to be discovered and said than can possibly be contained in a single book. I pray that it may stimulate further study, prayer, preaching, and writing on the Psalms.

May God give us tears of love as we pray and preach these imprecatory psalms. Many ministers have cast off these psalms and have abandoned this part of God's Word, with deadly results in the churches. I believe with all my heart that embracing and proclaiming anew the essential truths taught here will climax in the prosperity and advancement of the kingdom of God on the earth. When these holy prayers are again prayed in the Spirit and with understanding, there will come unsuspected power and glory to the church of Christ.

# Acknowledgments

In my march through the Psalms God has given me much help and encouragement through His people, making this project—though imperfect—a great joy. Along the way I have acquired an immense debt of gratitude and love to:

- *Paul Martin* and *Philip Martin,* who have taught me so much about the Psalms;
- *Joseph Baranyi* of Budapest, Hungary, whose many hours of computer work have been of incomputable value;
- *Jim and Gerry Blose* and *Ed Klotz,* whose cabins provided a quiet place to write;
- *Rudy and Etta DeJong,* whose home was open to me and my family during my studies at Westminster Seminary in California in 1983 and 1989;
- *Pastors Jorge Zamora* and *Earl Blackburn,* who organized seminars on the psalms of imprecation;
- *Dr. Robert Knight Rudolph,* my beloved professor (now with the Lord), whose teaching gave me the theological foundation to understand more of God's glory;
- *Ernest C. Reisinger,* for his commitment to see these truths go forth;
- *Cornerstone Bible Fellowship,* the faithful ones who stand with me and patiently lift me up in prayer;
- *Dr. Jay Adams,* Director of Advanced Studies at Westminster Seminary in California, whose vision for this book kept me going;
- *Chuck and Penny Klotz* and *Bill and Louise Wenger* of Carlisle, Pennsylvania, for unwavering love and encouragement;
- the three true "arrows" God graciously put in the hands of this warrior (Ps. 127): *Jonathan, Debbie,* and *David,* partners throughout this endeavor by their prayer, love, and support.

*Soli Deo Gloria!*

Break the teeth in their mouths, O God; tear out, O Lord, the fangs of the lions! Let them vanish like water that flows away; when they draw the bow, let their arrows be blunted. Like a slug melting away as it moves along, like a stillborn child, may they not see the sun. Before your pots can feel the heat of the thorns—whether they be green or dry—the wicked will be swept away. The righteous will be glad when they are avenged, when they bathe their feet in the blood of the wicked.

Psalm 58:6-10

For the sins of their mouths, for the words of their lips, let them be caught in their pride. For the curses and lies they utter, consume them in wrath, consume them till they are no more. Then it will be known to the ends of the earth that God rules over Jacob.

Psalm 59:12, 13

Pour out your wrath on them; let your fierce anger overtake them. May their place be deserted; let there be no one to dwell in their tents. For they persecute those you wound and talk about the pain of those you hurt. Charge them with crime upon crime; do not let them share in your salvation. May they be blotted out of the book of life and not be listed with the righteous.

Psalm 69:24-28

# 1

# Those Puzzling Prayers From the Psalms

Have you ever been puzzled by the Psalms? Many of these beautiful Hebrew poems are obviously prayers, and it doesn't seem natural to most of us merely to *read* them as if we were listening in on someone else's conversation with God. In times of joy or deep sorrow and confusion don't you frequently enter into the spirit of the Psalms and pray them as your own? But then, with your heart fully engaged in prayer, you come upon those phrases that seem so shocking—so diametrically opposed—to all you've been taught in Christian love and forbearance.

How are you to understand a prayer from Scripture that says, "Break the teeth in their mouths, O God" (Ps. 58:6) or "Let death take my enemies by surprise; let them go down alive to the grave" (Ps. 55:15)? That's strong language!

Have you wondered whether the psalmist's prayers, "May all my enemies be ashamed and dismayed; . . . may they perish in disgrace" (6:10; 83:17) are an expression of sinful revenge, as some writers say? Is he guilty of expressing worldly sentiments of revenge as in a newspaper classified ad I saw recently?

> Jilted? Stood up? Divorced? Fired? Whatever your meaningless memory, now you can wilt 'em away with a wilted bouquet! Just call Wilted Flowers, your therapeutic floral consultants, and put a little happiness in your hurt.

Do you think the psalmist is indulging such spiteful feelings?

Too many sincere Christians rush past such expressions as if shielding their faces from the heat of hatred, quickly moving on to other sections where they find more comfortable language. (There are so many *soothing* phrases in the Psalms!) But can that be a proper response to any part of God's Word? Or is it merely a cop-out?

The problem is bigger than many realize! The more carefully we look at the Psalms, the more we see that the prayers for vengeance are not a handful of side comments. They are not found in just a few isolated places so that we can overlook them and decide that it may not be worth our time to try to understand them. They pervade the book! Then we begin to recognize that other portions of the Old Testament express similar ideas. We even find them restated by our Lord and His apostles in the *New Testament!*

Have you who accept the Scripture as the only rule of faith and practice grappled with these issues? Have you who are called to handle correctly the word of truth sought to apprehend the truths taught here so as to be able to break this bread for God's people?

Serious Bible students have puzzled over these problems for centuries, so if you find yourself perplexed, don't be surprised. Some people have found it so difficult to understand these perplexing prayers that they have concluded that these segments were mistakenly included in the Word of God. But our doctrine of inspiration must lead us to expand our knowledge of God and His ways as we seek solutions to these deep questions. There *are* answers, and it is *our* business as followers of the Most High God to apply ourselves to understand His Word so that we will find them. What an exciting assignment is now set before us!

## Uniqueness of the Psalms

The book of Psalms is unique among the sixty-six books of the Bible in that it is a prayer book given to us by God. Later we'll discuss in more depth our need for this prayer book from God and how we are to use it in our Christian lives and preaching. For now let's recognize that giants of the church through the ages have found deep mines of truth here and that the hearts of New Testament believers today beat a responding "Amen" to its expressions of comfort, contrition, and praise.

John Calvin, the great theologian of the Reformation, wrote a very extensive commentary on this prayer book of the Bible. In the preface to his classic volumes on the Psalms the Reformer speaks of the heavenly doctrine in these prayers and stresses their importance for entering into "genuine and earnest prayer." His own experience of drawing near to God through these prayers is evident as he says,

> In short, as calling upon God is one of the principal means of securing safety, and as a better and more unerring rule for guiding us in this exercise cannot be found elsewhere than in the Psalms, it follows, that in proportion to the proficiency which a man shall have attained in understanding them, will be his knowledge of the most important part of celestial doctrine.[1]

These God-given prayers become, in effect, the pathway on which God leads us upward to Himself.

Our Lord Jesus Christ and His apostles used the Psalms constantly in teaching men to know God. The New Testament directly quotes the Old Testament approximately 283 times. An astounding 41 percent (116 of the 283) of all these Old Testament quotations are from the Psalms. According to the gospel records, Christ Himself alluded to the Psalms over fifty times. To know God truly and to be equipped to lead others to a knowledge of Him we must read, learn, and inwardly digest these prayers.

My own experience with these prayers has brought me many times to sense God's very presence. As my understanding of them deepened through much study, comparing Scripture with Scripture, my prayer life has begun to enter into the very prayers of Jesus Christ. I've also been enabled to preach these psalms with great joy. It is my earnest desire to help you to learn how to rejoice in praying and preaching the Psalms of the Prince of Peace.

### Questions for Thought and Discussion

1. In what ways are the Psalms unique?

2. What is the attitude of Christ and the New Testament writers toward the Psalms?

3. What comments and reactions have you heard others express with regard to the imprecatory psalms?

4. Begin to think how you may answer those who question the cries of vengeance found in the Psalms.

**Notes**

1. John Calvin, *Calvin's Commentaries* (Grand Rapids: Baker, 1981), 4:xxxvii.

Perhaps there is no part of the Bible that gives more perplexity and pain to its readers than this; perhaps nothing that constitutes a more plausible objection to the belief that the psalms are the productions of inspired men than the spirit of revenge which they sometimes seem to breathe and the spirit of cherished malice and implacableness which the writers seem to manifest.

Albert Barnes
*Notes, Critical, Explanatory and Practical on the Book of Psalms*


To some minds, these imprecatory psalms and passages are perhaps a more difficult obstacle than any other in the way of a settled confidence in the Divine inspiration of the Scriptures.

J. Sidlow Baxter
*Explore the Book*


All Scripture is God-breathed and is useful for teaching, rebuking, correcting and training in righteousness, so that the man of God may be thoroughly equipped for every good work.

Paul the apostle
2 Timothy 3:16-17

# 2

# *Are These Prayers the Oracles of God?*

The title of this chapter asks a fundamental question that must be settled before we can proceed: Are such prayers really from God? It is essential that we always approach Scripture with a biblical theology of inspiration. To examine any portion of Scripture with a reservation regarding its divine origin is perilous. We must see that we *cannot* base our acceptance of these psalms as the true Word of God upon our own response to them. Too many Christians have allowed instinctive feelings of repulsion or shock at the language to cause them to reject these words as Scripture.

Of course, many people do reject the Bible as the inspired Word of God. Some choose to blame their unbelief on the "inconsistency" they find in its pages, and they often cite the difference between the language of these psalms and the "spirit of love in the New Testament" as a case in point. When openly declared infidels repudiate the Psalms, we are hardly surprised. What does alarm us is to see professing Christians do the same. Let's look at what a few of them have said. You'll recognize some well-known and highly regarded names among the objectors, so be prepared!

## What Some Have Said

Bible scholars whose understanding of inspiration has been determined solely by human standards do not unduly alarm us when they call into question the divine origin of these particular

7

prayers. When a person's criterion for determining the canonicity of a certain passage is his own sense of good or evil, he will very *likely* reject at least some of the Psalms, along with other passages of Scripture. So when faced with the difficulties presented by the strongly worded curses of the Psalms, he or she may matter-of-factly conclude with John Bright that "we cannot demand that the Bible give us nothing but correct teachings and safe moral instruction and be offended at it when it does not."[1] Or as another, John J. Owen (not the Puritan), said of the psalms of imprecation, these "forms of expression are of such cold-blooded and malignant cruelty, as to preclude entertaining the idea for a moment that they were inspired of God."[2]

It stuns and saddens us, however, to see *evangelical* theologians whom we respect begin to whine and stumble when they approach the "justice psalms." But our belief in inspiration must not be shaken even when we hear "accepted authorities" attacking God's Word. On the contrary, we must certainly call into question the doctrine of Scripture held by anyone who reduces inspiration to mere religious insight. J. I. Packer helpfully points out the tragic fact that in modern theology

> Scripture is allowed a relative authority, based on the supposition that its authors, being men of insight, probably say much that is right; but this is in effect to deny to Scripture the authority which properly belongs to the words of a God who cannot lie. This modern view expressly allows for the possibility that sometimes the biblical writers, being children of their age, had their minds so narrowed by conditioning factors in their environment that, albeit unwittingly, they twisted and misstated God's truth. And when any particular biblical idea cuts across what men today like to think, modern Protestants are fatally prone to conclude that this is a case in point, where the Bible saw things crooked, but we today, differently conditioned, can see them straight.[3]

We should be appalled in this light to learn that *Halley's Bible Handbook*, a standard Christian reference work, states unapologetically that these psalms are not God's pronouncements of His wrath on the wicked; but are the prayers of a man for vengeance on his enemies, just the opposite of Jesus' teaching that we should love our enemies.[4]

This widely recognized best seller proceeds to justify its heresy with the theory that

in Old Testament times God, in measure, for expedience' sake, accommodated Himself to Men's Ideas. In New Testament times God began to deal with men according to His Own Ideas [*sic*].[5]

This explanation unashamedly teaches that the psalmist's prayers are in disobedience to God. Another unfortunate opinion has been propounded by *The Pulpit Commentary*, when commenting on Psalm 35: "So with this and other imprecatory psalms, they give us, not God's precept, but man's defective prayers."[6] Can a disciple of Christ accept such a conclusion?

I was disappointed to find even the thought-provoking C. S. Lewis in the camp of protestors. He actually speaks of these psalms as "devilish" and "diabolical"! Initially, we may feel confused when we see this venerated author using such awful adjectives to refer to Scripture. But when his words finally penetrate, we become outraged! No wonder Cornelius Van Til said,

One would think he reads a modern humanist rather than an evangelical Christian when he hears Lewis speak of the "devilish" character of the psalmist's sentiments as, e.g., expressed in Psalm 109.[7]

Lewis falls into the trap of judging the Psalms by his own instincts and ends by condemning them:

The hatred is there—festering, gloating, undisguised—and also we should be wicked if we in any way condoned or approved it, or (worse still) used it to justify similar passions in ourselves.[8]

Although he seeks to "understand" the wickedness of the psalmist's enemies that caused the cries to God for vengeance, his conclusion with regard to the psalmist's prayers is *"They are indeed devilish."*[9]

If our quest for help in understanding these psalms leads us to the *Word Bible Commentary*, which claims to be "a showcase of the best in evangelical critical scholarship for a new generation,"[10] we are again led astray. Here Peter C. Craigie explains the "problematic passages" in the Psalms as

> the real and natural reactions to the experience of evil and pain, and though the sentiments are in themselves evil, they are a part of the life of the soul which is bared before God in worship and prayer.[11]

He takes these cries of anguish as expressions of the psalmist's hatred and sin toward his enemies and says: "The psalmist may hate his oppressor; God hates the oppression. Thus the words of the psalmist are often natural and spontaneous, not always pure and good."[12]

By using such words he denies that these psalms are a part of God's pure law. "The words of the Lord are pure words" (Ps. 12:6; see also Pss. 19:8; 119:140, ASV, 1901.) Finally, Craigie states blatantly that "*these Psalms are not the oracles of God.*"[13]

It is important that we know what commentators have said. It is even possible that some people in our own congregations may draw the very same conclusions. But we must seek a *biblical* understanding of these passages!

### Possible Reasons for These Statements and Where They Lead

Everyone seems to be in agreement that these psalms, often called psalms of imprecation (or cursing), are very difficult to understand. But while we seek to extend the utmost courtesy and benefit of doubt to Christian brothers, we must disagree radically with many of their conclusions. The fact that something in the Word of God is beyond our comprehension is *not* grounds for denying or even questioning its inspiration.

Some who criticize these psalms are obviously being guided by purely human feelings. They claim that these prayers are contrary to the higher feelings of *human nature*, that they go against the common sentiments of compassion and therefore are evil. This is a classic instance in which the church of Jesus Christ needs to be reminded of the godhood of God! Our minds were not given to create a god after our ideas and desires. We are not free to determine right and wrong according to our own "higher instincts" or judgment. We must humbly acknowledge God as our Creator. It is He who reveals to us who He is and how we may know what is truth. Even our "higher instincts" as man are as trash beneath the feet of our holy God. To make ourselves the judge of good and evil is to take impudently the place of God. We may never do that in any context. We must never presume to sit in judgment on God!

Others who find fault with these psalms undoubtedly have good intentions and may even have a commendable but misplaced jealousy for the purity of God's honor. What else could have moved the famous C. I. Scofield to determine that Old Testament prayers for vengeance are a "cry unsuited to the Church"?[14] Do we imagine ourselves holier than God? Wrong ideas of God and His honor have led many men to become what I would term "evangelical plastic surgeons." They have made it their job to "clean up" God's Word according to their own ideas of what is proper.

Their methods are really very similar to those of the modernists in the early years of the twentieth century, whose approach to Jesus was to exclaim, "Jesus is wonderful!" And we feel a joy of kindred spirit! . . . until we hear their next words: "But we can't accept His miracles, virgin birth, and claims of deity." When we ask them, "Why not?" they respond, "They're not compatible with our Christianity!" They may profess ever so loudly the name of Christ, may still call upon His name in prayer and seek to walk in outward conformity to His Word, but in reality they have put themselves in the place that belongs to God alone. They have forgotten that it is He who must determine what Christianity is and what is suited for His church.

If you presume to take God's place, audaciously deciding what He is to say and how He is to say it, you have placed yourself over God! We lack the authority to judge Him. Nor are our efforts needed to defend Him. His honor stands far above any of our efforts to secure it.

*What Is Our Response?*

As God's people who receive His Word as truth (and especially we ministers who proclaim that Word), it is not our calling to justify all the acts and words of God's people in Scripture. Obviously, they were sinful men who fell into many grievous errors. But the Psalms are not just words and acts of men. They are part of God's revelation of Himself and His attributes, and they are reaffirmed by the New Testament as the authoritative Word of God and of His Christ.

Do we fully realize that the psalms these evangelical plastic surgeons reject as being "unsuited"—"unworthy" for the church —are the very psalms Christ used to testify about Himself? In his 1959 master's thesis at Westminster Theological Seminary, Harry Mennega pointed out that

> the New Testament appears not in the least embarrassed with the Old Testament imprecations; on the contrary, it quotes freely from them as authoritative statements with which to support an argument. The New Testament not only quotes passages which, though themselves not imprecations, are found in a Psalm with an imprecatory section; but also, and this is more remarkable, it quotes with approval the imprecations themselves.[15]

A very clear example of the New Testament's quoting with approval an imprecation from the Psalms is given at the very initiation of the New Testament church. In Acts 1 Peter says, "For . . . it is written in the book of Psalms, 'May his place be deserted; let there be no one to dwell in it,' and, 'May another take his place of leadership.'" These two quotations are taken from two of the most "notorious" of all the imprecatory psalms: 69 and 109. They are applied to Judas who betrayed the Lord Jesus. Peter is here quoting an invocation of judgment and a curse against the betrayer of God's Anointed One.

William Binnie, Professor of Church History at the Free Church College in Aberdeen, Scotland, in 1886, interjected some interesting comments into this discussion:

> The frequency with which the Old Testament Scriptures are cited by our blessed Lord and the writers of the New Testament . . . has

always, and justly, been regarded as a strong testimony to the plenary authority of the ancient Scriptures. This being so, the fact is remarkable that the psalms under discussion have been counted worthy of an eminent share in this honour. The sixty-ninth, for example, which bears more of the imprecatory character than any other except the hundred-and-ninth, is expressly quoted in five separate places, besides being alluded to in several places more.[16]

More and more we see what a serious matter we have before us. The close interweaving of the New Testament with these most difficult psalms stresses their value for our churches today. Remember that it is *God* who gives His Word. Our role is to receive, love, and obey it. The very words that many condemn as dishonoring to God are, in fact, promoting His honor. Could it be true that these psalms about which preachers refuse to preach are the ones our people need most to hear? Let's consider the challenge put to us by one of the greatest preachers of the twentieth century, David Martyn Lloyd-Jones, in one of his penetrating sermons:

> Look at the psalmist. Look at some of those imprecatory psalms. What are they? There is nothing wrong with them. It's just the zeal of the psalmist. He's grieved and troubled because these people are not honoring God as they should be. That's his supreme concern.[17]

And this must be the supreme concern of every Christian! God's honor must be expressed as *He* prescribes.

### What We May Not Do

The essence of what many, perhaps unwittingly, have done is to question the authority of God's Word. Long ago Eve began this evil tradition of questioning God's Word. Since that time, and as a result of that fall, sinners have refused to recognize God as the supreme authority and have tried to snatch this authority for themselves.

As true followers of Christ and leaders of others in His way, we repent of our instinctive rebellion and determine to reverence God's Word *even when* we cannot understand its meaning or how it relates to the rest of biblical teaching. God clearly tells us through the apostle Paul that "all Scripture is God-breathed and is useful for teaching, rebuking, correcting and training in right- eousness . . ." (2 Tim. 3:16). This statement does not allow us the freedom to doubt the inspiration of the Scriptures, or any part of them, for any reason. We may not say, "I think God's Word should sound like this," and make deletions or changes based on our whims. Nor are we at liberty to repudiate a part because we find it beyond our puny comprehension.

Even Peter as an apostle was not at liberty to determine the inspiration of a given revelation by his own understanding. He was inspired by the same Holy Spirit who inspired Paul's writ- ings to record: "Our dear brother Paul also wrote you with the wisdom that God gave him. . . . His letters contain some things hard to understand" (2 Pet. 3:15-16). Hard for *Peter?* But he af- firms at the same time (v. 16) that they form a part of God's Word along with "other scriptures." This verse also conveys a warning to us in its report of ignorant and unstable people who were distorting those difficult words. Let us not follow their example and be betrayed into a denial of God's own Holy Word! The responsibility of Christians who teach others is great. We must never lower the standard of inspiration. The Word of God stands above the best reason and wisdom of men.

### Why Do We Accept All of the Psalms as Scripture?

From Old Testament times the recorded words of David were acknowledged to be divinely inspired. The witness of the Old Testament is clear in 2 Samuel 23:1-2:

> These are the last words of David: "The oracle of David son of Jesse, the oracle of the man exalted by the Most High, the man anointed by the God of Jacob, Israel's singer of songs: 'The Spirit of the Lord spoke through me; his word was on my tongue.'"

Jesus' witness to the authenticity of these psalms as Scripture is unmistakable: "The Holy Spirit inspired David to say: 'The Lord said to my Lord: Sit here at my right side until I put your enemies under your feet'" (Mark 12:36). In addition, the apostles cite the Psalms as Scripture through the inspiration of the Holy Spirit. Listen to Peter: "Brothers, the Scripture had to be fulfilled which the Holy Spirit spoke long ago through the mouth of David concerning Judas who served as guide for those who arrested Jesus" (Acts 1:16).

Furthermore, the Spirit has given conclusive verification of the Psalms by the witness of His church through the centuries:

> The Psalms have been received by the church of God in past generations, without any dissentient voice, as a book of that Holy Scripture, of which Christ declared that it "cannot be broken."[18]

As such they were given by the Spirit of God, and as such they were accepted, used, and honored by the Lord Jesus Christ.

To take some of the very passages quoted by our Lord and call them *not the oracles of God, unsuited for the church,* and *devilish* is a clear denial of the inspiration of the Word of God. Furthermore, it reflects upon His deity. If He commended "devilish" teaching, could He be God? To reject any word given by the Holy Spirit and call evil what God has given to us for our profit is an abomination to God. Let's take care to examine ourselves in this regard. Dietrich Bonhoeffer, a martyr of this century, cautions us:

> Has it not become terrifyingly clear again and again that we are no longer obedient to the Bible? We are more fond of our own thoughts than of the thoughts of the Bible.[19]

The rejection of any part of God's Word is a rejection of the giver of that Word, God Himself. Our response should rather be that of C. H. Spurgeon who, commenting on Psalm 109, said,

> Truly this is one of the hard places of Scripture, a passage which the soul trembles to read, yet as it is a Psalm unto God, and given by inspiration, it is not ours to sit in judgment upon it, but to bow our ear to what God the Lord would speak to us therein.[20]

In the face of all argument we must confess unwaveringly that all of the Psalms *are* indeed the inspired Word of God. This commitment of trust in God's Word is an absolute prerequisite for a proper understanding of that Word. The Spirit of God spoke through David in such a way that his words came not from himself but from the mouth of God. Let us beg that same Spirit's help in comprehending these psalms of imprecation. Only then will we discern how they harmonize with the New Testament command to love our enemies. This understanding cannot be merely for our own private profit but for the church of Jesus Christ at large, as God gives us utterance to preach these psalms with a fresh vision.

### *Renew Your Covenant of Trust*

Before you read more, renew your covenant of trust in God's Word. Agree with the Lord Jesus Christ that David spoke and wrote in the Spirit. (See Matt. 22:43; Mark 12:36; Acts 1:16; 4:25; Heb. 4:7.) This will require humility and trust: humility to forsake your own judgment as the final authority, and trust in God's Word even when you can't understand. You will find that your study will then be transformed from the simple analysis of some ancient prayers to an increased knowledge of God that will draw forth fervent praise to the One who reveals Himself to you in these cries for justice.

Having made this covenant of trust in God's Word, you are ready to go forward. You are in a state of heart and mind to ask and answer questions such as: How can these curses be understood as agreeing with the New Testament command to love our enemies? Do these psalms show the religion of the Old Testament saints to be defective? Is the anger in these prayers sinful? Who is speaking in these psalms? Can these prayers be prayed and preached today? Is it ever right to rejoice over the downfall of our enemies?

As we seek by the illumination of the Holy Spirit to understand the psalms of imprecation, these are some of the questions we must answer for our own profit as well as that of others. Let us pray with the psalmist: "Open thou mine eyes, that I may behold wondrous things out of thy law"; "In thy light we shall see light" (Pss. 119:18; 36:9).

## Questions for Thought and Discussion

1. Can we consent to the idea that portions of the Psalms are merely incorrect opinions of human authors, albeit "inspired" accounts of such? How would you answer someone who holds such a view?

2. How is a person's grasp of and profit from the whole of Scripture affected when he or she allows the authority of any one part of it to be undercut?

3. What are some examples of other scriptural teachings or actions of God that may seem to our minds wrong but in which we must submit to God who defines the good?

(The use of the Psalms by Christ in the New Testament will be of invaluable help in dealing with questions raised against these portions of the Psalms. See Appendix 4.)

### Notes

1. John Bright, *The Authority of the Old Testament* (Grand Rapids: Baker, 1975), p. 236.
2. John J. Owen, "The Imprecatory Psalms," *The Bibliotheca Sacra and American Biblical Repository* 13 (July, 1856):552.
3. J. I. Packer, "Introductory Essay," in James Buchanan, *The Doctrine of Justification* (London: Banner of Truth, 1961), p. 5.
4. Henry H. Halley, *Halley's Bible Handbook* (Minneapolis: Grason, 1962), p. 191.
5. Ibid.
6. H. D. M. Spence and Joseph S. Exell, eds., *The Pulpit Commentary*, vol. 8, *The Psalms* (Grand Rapids: Eerdmans, 1962), p. 270.
7. Cornelius Van Til, *Christian Theistic Ethics* (Nutley, N.J.: Presbyterian and Reformed, 1980), p. 85.
8. C. S. Lewis, *Reflections on the Psalms* (New York: Harcourt Brace Jovanovich, 1958), p. 22.
9. Ibid., p. 25, emphasis added.
10. *Word Biblical Commentary* (Waco, Tex.: Word, 1983), back cover of book.
11. Ibid., p. 41.
12. Ibid.

13. Ibid., emphasis added.

14. *Scofield Reference Bible* (New York: Oxford University Press, 1917), p. 599.

15. Harry Mennega, "The Ethical Problem of the Imprecatory Psalms" (master's thesis, Westminster Theological Seminary, 1959), p. 38.

16. William Binnie, *The Psalms, Their History, Teachings and Use* (London: Hodder and Stoughton, 1886), pp. 276-77.

17. David Martyn Lloyd-Jones, sermon on evangelism delivered in Carlisle, Pa., 1969.

18. James Dick, "The 'Imprecatory Psalms,'" *Psalm-Singers' Conference* (Belfast: Fountain Printing, 1903), p. 87.

19. Martin Kuske, *The Old Testament as the Book of Christ* (Philadelphia: Westminster Press, 1976), p. 21.

20. C. H. Spurgeon, *Treasury of David.*(London: Passmore and Alabaster, 1882), 5:157.

According to the witness of the Bible, David is, as the anointed king of the chosen people of God, a prototype of Jesus Christ. What happens to him happens to him for the sake of the one who is in him and who is said to proceed from him, namely Jesus Christ. And he is not unaware of this, but "being therefore a prophet, and knowing that God had sworn with an oath to him that he would set one of his descendants upon his throne, he foresaw and spoke of the resurrection of the Christ" (Acts 2:30f.). David was a witness to Christ in his office, in his life, and in his words. The New Testament says even more. In the Psalms of David the promised Christ himself already speaks (Hebrews 2:12; 10:5) or, as may also be indicated, the Holy Spirit (Hebrews 3:7). These same words which David spoke, therefore, the future Messiah spoke through him. The prayers of David were prayed also by Christ. Or better, Christ himself prayed them through his forerunner David.

Dietrich Bonhoeffer
*Psalms: The Prayer Book of the Bible*


David, for example, was a type and spokesman of Christ, and the imprecatory Psalms are expressions of the infinite justice of the God-man, of His indignation against wrong-doing, of His compassion for the wronged. They reveal the feelings of His heart and the sentiments of His mind regarding sin.

J. H. Webster
*The Psalms in Worship*

# 3

# Who Is Praying
# These Psalms?

The question Who is praying for God to destroy His enemies? is really the critical issue with the imprecatory psalms. If *you* were to ask God to destroy your personal enemy, that would be in essence cursing that enemy and, therefore, sinful. But if the King of Peace asks God to destroy *His* enemies, that is another matter! (Read through Pss. 101 and 18.)

Are the Psalms merely a record of the emotionally charged prayers of individuals who lived thousands of years ago? All Scripture is against such a view. Certainly they are of far greater grandeur and worth than that. But whose prayers are they, really?

## Not Our Own Personal Prayers

Have you ever been praying in the words of a psalm and suddenly found yourself unable to continue? Sometimes the words stop us short! How can I cry out before God that "the Lord has dealt with me according to my righteousness"? The psalmist goes on to say,

> According to the cleanness of my hands he has rewarded me. For I have kept the ways of the Lord; I have not done evil by turning from my God. All his laws are before me; I have not turned away from his decrees. I have been blameless before him and have kept myself from sin. The Lord has rewarded me according to my

righteousness, according to the cleanness of my hands in his sight (Ps. 18:20-24).

These words *cannot* be my words personally or those of anyone I know. We feel uneasy even reading these words aloud, much less making them our prayer to the Lord who knows the sinfulness of our hearts.

As a matter of fact, it's difficult to understand how *David* could pray this way. Some in the congregations I've served have struggled with this problem and have come to me for help. Some of their concerns may coincide with your own: "Even if David wrote this Psalm before his 'great sin' with Bathsheba, he couldn't have been *this* righteous, could he?" I have reminded them that David admitted to being a sinner from birth (Ps. 51:5) as are all born of Adam. Others have asked: "Did David not recognize his sin? These sound like the words of a perfect man." That fact jumps off the page at us as we read this psalm.

Or take the words of the passion and crucifixion of Christ found in Psalm 22:

> Dogs have surrounded me; a band of evil men has encircled me, they have pierced my hands and my feet. I can count all my bones; people stare and gloat over me. They divide my garments among them and cast lots for my clothing (vv. 16-18).

Have you ever asked yourself how David wrote this? We are never told that he experienced any of these things, although he did have many *other* difficulties. We know from the New Testament that the Lord Jesus made these words His very own during His suffering on earth. But in what sense could David write them? And how much less do these prayers fit *me!*

In the same way, when our minds function well and our hearts feel the weight of our own sin, to call for God to destroy the wicked enemies with the psalmist causes us to falter. *I am wicked, too! How can I use such language as my own?* Can we ask God that our personal enemies would have their "eyes darkened so they cannot see, and their backs be bent forever"? (Ps. 69:23). What fearful words! Should *we* take it upon ourselves to ask God, "Pour out your wrath on them; let your fierce anger overtake them" (Ps. 69:24)?

We must be careful not to make the Psalms our own personal prayers according to our changeful moods. But neither are they merely Jewish prayers of long ago for us to read selectively according to the whim of our emotions. They are obviously a central part of the Word of God and, as such, are worthy of careful attention. We must come to understand them as Christ and His apostles understood them.

### The Psalms in the Life of Our Lord

We do not approach the Psalms without light or help. On the contrary, we have the entire New Testament writings to help us understand them. The Psalter occupied an enormous place in the life of our Lord. He used it as His prayer book in the Jewish synagogue during His whole life. It was His songbook in all the temple festivals. He sang from it after the last supper.

Did Jesus simply use the book of Psalms as other Jews of His day did? Have you observed the Lord's personal relationship to the Psalms? He quoted the Psalter not merely as prophecy; He actually spoke the Psalms as His own words!

We especially notice this close identification with the Psalms when we give careful attention to His awesome cries from the cross. He gave up His life with the words of the Psalms on His lips: "Father, into your hands I commit my spirit" (31:5); "My God, my God, why have you forsaken me?" (22:1). His words of anguish, "I am thirsty," echo Psalms 69:21 and 22:15, and His cry of triumph, "It is finished!" reminds us of Psalm 22:31. ("He has done it": the Septuagint of Psalm 22 uses the same verb that Jesus does.) In his death Jesus quoted the Psalms not as some ancient authority that He adapted for His own use, but as His very own words—the words of the Lord's Anointed which, as David's Son, He truly was.

When we look diligently, we find that the Lord Christ's use of the Psalms as His own words was not peculiar to His time of suffering on the cross. Throughout His ministry He made the

words of the Psalms His own. Jesus foretells what *He* will say as
the Judge in the final day when He quotes the words of Psalm 6:8:
"Then I will tell them plainly, 'I never knew you. Away from me,
you evildoers'" (Matt. 7:23). He speaks the words of Psalm 35:19
and 69:4 as referring directly to Himself: "They hated me without
reason" (John 15:25). (For further instances, compare Matt. 7:23
with Ps. 6:8; Matt. 21:13 with Ps. 118:26; John 13:18 with Ps. 41:9;
Matt. 16:27 with Ps. 62:12.)

### The Apostles' Witness

How Jesus' apostles regarded His connection to the Psalms is
decisive. They were constantly in His company during His ministry, being taught by Him, and afterwards being given special
illumination and inspiration for recording His deeds and words
(cf. John 14:26; 15:26; 16:13.) They give clear witness in the gospels
to His repeatedly speaking the words of the Psalms as His very
own.

The apostles and New Testament writers give us further enlightenment in their epistles. Hebrews 10:5 is a fascinating case
in point:

> When Christ came into the world, he said: "Sacrifice and offering
> you did not desire, but a body you prepared for me; with burnt
> offerings and sin offerings you were not pleased. Then I said,
> 'Here I am—it is written about me in the scroll—I have come to
> do your will, O God.'"

(This is a direct quote of the Septuagint version of Ps. 40:6-8.)

How can we know that Jesus said this? It is nowhere recorded
in the gospels as a statement of Jesus'. This exciting passage
provides the key to the apostles' understanding of the Psalms.
Three times it refers these words to Jesus (vv. 5, 8, 9). It tells us in
essence that Christ came into the world speaking the words of the
Psalms as His own.

Notice a similar instance in Hebrews 2:11-12:

Jesus is not ashamed to call them brothers. He says, "I will declare your name to my brothers; in the presence of the congregation I will sing your praises."

Here again we have words from a psalm (22:22) attributed to Jesus, though there is never a mention in the gospels of His having spoken these words while on earth. These two passages reflect clearly that the apostles believed Christ is speaking in the Psalms.

This New Testament understanding of Christ in the Psalms is fundamental to praying and preaching these psalms. The psalmist cries out for God to execute justice and judgment. Christ came to establish His kingdom and to extend mercy to all the earth. But let us never forget that Jesus *will* come again to execute judgment on the wicked.

## The "I" of the Psalms Is Identified

Even in our brief look at New Testament teaching we see a clear pattern. Further intense investigation bears out that the "I," the author of the Psalms, is Christ Himself. His is the great voice we hear in the Psalms crying out in prayer to God the Father. The Old Testament scholar E. W. Hengstenberg, part of the rear guard of orthodoxy in Germany in the nineteenth century, succinctly remarked of "the so-called vindictive Psalms,"

> It is precisely the most severe of these which are applied to Christ, and considered as spoken by him, and are therefore pronounced worthy of him.[1]

The Spirit of Christ was in the psalmists, speaking through them centuries before He came to earth as the long-awaited Messiah.

There are varying ways in which the Psalms speak of the Christ. In some we hear the Father talking to the Son, such as in Psalm 2:7: "You are my son; today I have become your Father." In others Christ is presented as the Good Shepherd (compare Ps. 23 with John 10). He is the King (Ps. 24), the Second Adam (perfect man—Ps. 1) and the Head of His church (compare Ps. 8 with Heb. 2).[2] Christ is Lord of all the Psalms!

### What About David?

Let's take a closer look at David, since it is logical to wonder about his role in this light. Our Lord said that David spoke by the Spirit (Matt. 22:43). Hebrews 4:7 even uses *David's name* as if it were a *title* of the Psalms: ". . . saying in David so long a time afterward . . ." (ASV, 1901). David is the principal human author of the Psalms not only because he penned the majority of them, but also because the whole of the Psalms are written "in the ink" of the Lord's Anointed—the Christ.

The Psalms are attributed to David not only by seventy-two superscriptions of the Psalms themselves but also by the New Testament. (See Acts 1:16; 2:25; 4:25; Rom. 4:6; 11:9; Heb. 4:7.) In some cases the New Testament writers ascribe to David psalms that have no title indicating Davidic authorship. This is not a careless generalizing but a careful instructing in the truth that the psalmists wrote their songs *in the spirit of* the Anointed One of God.

Franz Delitzsch makes a very insightful observation in this regard:

> As the New Testament Canon contains no writings of the apostles before the day of Pentecost, so the Old Testament Canon contains none of the songs of David prior to his anointing. Only when he has become "the Anointed of the God of Jacob" is he the sweet singer of Israel, on whose tongue is the word of Jehovah (2 Sam. 23:1).[3]

(The Greek equivalent of the Hebrew word for "Anointed One" is "the Christ.")

Dietrich Bonhoeffer, martyred under the Nazis during the last days of World War II, adds this:

> According to the witness of the Bible, David is, as the anointed king of the chosen people of God, a prototype of Jesus Christ. What happens to him happens to him for the sake of the one who is in him; and who is said to proceed from him, namely Jesus Christ. And he is not unaware of this, but "being therefore a prophet, and knowing that God had sworn with an oath to him that he would set one of his descendants upon his throne, he

foresaw and spoke of the resurrection of the Christ" (Acts 2:30ff). David was a witness to Christ in his office, in his life, and in his words. The New Testament says even more. In the Psalms of David the promised Christ Himself already speaks (Hebrews 2:11, 12; 10:5). These same words which David spoke, therefore, the future Messiah spoke through him. The prayers of David were prayed also by Christ. Or better, Christ himself prayed them through His forerunner David.[4]

We do not argue that all of the Psalms were written by David or that the New Testament places the entire Psalter on the lips of Christ but that the entire Psalter is bound up with the name of David and of David's greater Son, Jesus Christ.[5] David, by the Spirit of Christ in him, speaks far beyond his own understanding and experience. He anticipates the coming, suffering, deliverance, and exaltation of his Son and Lord—Jesus, the Christ.

These are invaluable truths for us to understand and communicate to others. A christological understanding of the Psalms will enlighten for God's people the whole prayer life of Jesus Christ. His prayers have bearing on our lives daily.

### The Converse Issue

As we begin to hear the Psalms coming from the lips and heart of the Lord Jesus, a question unfailingly arises concerning the other face of the coin in our experience: not *perfection*, but *guilt!* I remember well grappling with this issue. And such a struggle is apparently a common progression in learning. In the seminars where I've had the privilege of assisting others to recognize and preach Christ in the Psalms, it has not been uncommon to hear someone ask reflectively, "What about the psalms of penitence, then? How are we to understand those?"

Let me begin to answer this question with some well-chosen words from a book I received as a gift from my good friend David Straub, who knew that I was doing research on the Psalms. This remarkable christological commentary on the Psalms written by George Horne, Bishop of Norwich in the early eighteenth century, had caught the attention of C. H. Spurgeon. If you're unfamiliar with Horne, it might be helpful to know that Spurgeon, in his *Commenting and Commentaries*, recommends Horne as "among the best of our English writers on this part of Scripture."[6]

In the preface to his commentary Bishop Horne gives this instruction regarding the Psalms that speak of personal sins and guiltiness before God:

> In some of the Psalms, David appears as one suffering for his sins. When man speaks of sin, he speaks of what is his own; and therefore, every Psalm, where sin is confessed to be the cause of sorrow, belongs originally and properly to us, as fallen sons of Adam, like David, and all other men. . . . Sometimes, indeed, it happens, that we meet with heavy complaints of the number and burden of sins, in Psalms, from which passages are quoted in the New Testament as uttered by our Redeemer, in which there seems to be no change of person from beginning to end. . . . *The solution of this difficulty . . . is this: that Christ in the day of his passion, standing charged with the sin and guilt of his people, speaks of such their sin and guilt, as if they were his own, appropriating to himself those debts, for which, in the capacity of a surety, he had made himself responsible.*[7]

Bishop Horne also provides an enlightening bit of Old Testament Jewish history to substantiate his point:

> The lamb, which, under the law, was offered for sin, took the name "guilt," because the guilt contracted by the offerer, was transferred to that innocent creature, and typically expiated by its blood. Was not this exactly the case, in truth and reality, with the Lamb of God? . . . If from his circumcision to his crucifixion he "bore our sins in his own body;" why should it be thought strange, that he should confess them, on our behalf, with his own mouth?[8]

Consider also the words of another commentator who has thought through these difficulties. E. C. Olsen, in his *Meditations in the Book of Psalms*, says:

> I am particularly impressed with the 5th verse of this 69th Psalm, where the Lord said, "O God, thou knowest my foolishness; and my sins are not hid from thee." For two thousand years no man who has had any respect for his intellect, has dared charge our Lord Jesus with sin. But some might ask, What do you mean when

you say our Lord is the speaker in this verse? Just this: the fact of Calvary is not a sham or mirage. It is an actual fact. Christ making atonement for sin was a reality. The New Testament declares that He who knew no sin was made sin for us that we might be made the righteousness of God in Him. As Christ restored that which He took not away, that is, restored to us a righteousness which we never had, so Christ had to take your sins and mine, your foolishness and mine. These sins became such an integral part of Him that He called them "my sins, and my foolishness." Our Lord was the substitute for the sinner. He had to take the sinner's place and, in so doing, He took upon Himself all of the sinner's sin. In the 53rd chapter of Isaiah it is written, "Surely he hath borne our griefs, and carried our sorrows . . . and the Lord hath laid on him the iniquity of us all." The iniquity of us all was laid upon Christ. He bore our sins "in his own body on the tree." Can you fathom that? When you do, you will understand the mystery of the gospel.[9]

When *David* speaks of sin in the Psalms it is clearly his own personal guilt. How, then, can the sinless Lord Christ pray this prayer for forgiveness? When our *Lord Christ* "was made sin," it was his taking upon himself the guilt and sin of His people. He intercedes before the Father for David's sin and mine. He suffered "the just for the unjust," bearing the wrath of God as if He were the sinner. In the words of the apostle Paul: "God made him who had no sin to be sin for us, so that in him we might become the righteousness of God" (2 Cor. 5:21).

Jonathan Edwards, that genius of American theologians, powerfully instructed his congregation at Northampton about Christ's identity with His people. In 1738 he extolled the love of his Lord with these words:

> His elect were, from all eternity, dear to him as the apple of his eye. He looked upon them so much as himself, that he regarded their concerns as his, and their interests as his own; *and he has even made their guilt as his, by a gracious assumption of it to himself, that it might be looked upon as his own,* through that divine imputation in virtue of which they are treated as innocent, while he suffers for them.[10]

Several hymn writers have expressed this truth in beautiful poetic language:

> Arise, my soul arise,
> Shake off thy guilty fears:
> The bleeding sacrifice
> In thy behalf appears:
> Before the throne my surety stands,
> My name is written on his hands.
>
> Charles Wesley

> I lay my sins on Jesus,
> The spotless Lamb of God;
> He bears them all, and frees us
> From the accursed load:
> I bring my guilt to Jesus,
> To wash my crimson stains
> White in his blood most precious,
> Till not a spot remains.
>
> Horatius Bonar

Surely the prophecy of Isaiah speaks profound truth when it tells us the suffering servant "was numbered with the transgressors"!

Before we leave this point let me encourage those of you who are teachers by sharing with you some of the exciting results I've seen from preaching these truths. In the flock to which I minister many of God's people have given thanks for this New Testament view of the Psalms. Apprehending the Psalms as the prayers of the Lord Jesus has broken their hearts in a fresh way over their own sin. One lady said, "Nothing has ever humbled me so much as hearing the voice of my blessed Lord Jesus, the Creator and Sustainer of heaven and earth, cry out in prayer to His Father in the Psalms for deliverance from the agonies that *my* sins brought upon His holy soul." May many more in churches across our land be moved to bow low before our great God and turn in repentance from their sins as we perceive the Psalms in this way!

We believe that Jesus, the Second Adam and true man, unceasingly and acceptably mediates for us, the fallen Adams. We believe that the Mouth of the body speaks, and though the body is sinful, Christ Himself never transgressed. His perfect righteous-ness is the guarantee that He is heard in our defense. The Head performs His loving ministry of pleading unceasingly for the forgiveness of the sins of the body, of which David and we are a part.

## Not a New Concept

In many circles a handful of psalms are classified as "messi-anic" (foretelling Christ and His work) while the bulk are rele-gated to an inferior category. Tremper Longman III, Associate Professor at Westminster Theological Seminary in Philadelphia, in his book, *How to Read the Psalms*, breaks down this superficial distinction and opens a window that sheds more light:

> The term "messianic psalm" may be used in one of two ways. In a general sense, a messianic psalm is simply a psalm which anticipates the Messiah. We will soon see that all the psalms are messianic in this sense. Some people, though, believe that a few psalms are messianic in the narrow sense. That is, some psalms are prophetic and have no direct message of significance for the Old Testament period. They only predict the coming Messiah. . . . While no psalm is exclusively messianic in the narrow sense, all the psalms look forward to Jesus Christ.[11]

The true messianic understanding of the Psalms is not a change in interpretation but an explanation of their original sense. David was writing as a prophet (2 Sam. 23:2; Acts 2:30). But he was more than a prophet; he was also the king of Israel and as such prayed and wrote for the people of God. Therefore, we must understand his prayers as *words of the Anointed of God*, the Christ, who is Prophet, Priest, and King (cf. Ps. 110).

This is not a new concept for the church. In his helpful little volume on the Psalms Andrew Bonar comments on the early church's view:

> Now, in the early ages, men full of the thoughts of Christ could never read the Psalms without being reminded of their Lord. They probably had no system or fixed theory as to all the Psalms referring to Christ; but still, unthinkingly, we might say, they

found their thoughts wandering to their Lord, as the one Person in whom these breathings, these praises, these desires, these hopes, these deep feelings, found their only true and full realization. Hence, Augustine (Psalm 58) said to his hearers, as he expounded to them this book, that "The voice of Christ and His Church was well-nigh the only voice to be heard in the Psalms.... We ought to recognize His voice in all the Psalms."[12]

My treasured commentary on the Psalms by George Horne gives further corroboration of the history of this understanding:

> The primitive Fathers ... are unexceptionable witnesses to us of this matter of fact, that such a method of expounding the Psalms, built upon the practice of the apostles in their writings and preachings, did universally prevail in the church from the beginning. They, who have ever looked into St. Augustine, know, that he pursues this plan invariably, treating of the Psalms as proceeding from the mouth of Christ, or of the church, or of both, considered as one mystical person. The same is true of Jerome, Ambrose, Arnobius, Cassidore, Hilary, and Prosper. . . . But what is very observable, Tertullian, who flourished at the beginning of the third century, mentions it, as if it were then an allowed point in the church, that almost all the Psalms are spoken in the person of Christ, being addressed by the Son to the Father, that is, by Christ to God.[13]

Horne additionally comments that even the solution to the difficulty of understanding the psalms that speak of "my sin," as we heard him explain above, is "given and continually insisted on in the writings of the Fathers."[14]

The imprecatory psalms in particular have been historically understood as being the voice of Christ. In 1907 J. H. Webster wrote regarding this kind of psalm:

> It has been well said that "Christ Himself is the best key to the Psalms." It does not surprise us to learn that the Apostolic Church regarded them, even the imprecatory, as the voice of Christ, or that Augustine and Luther referred the imprecatory ones exclusively to Him. Certainly the passages from them quoted by Christ and His Apostles, whose profound insight into the Scriptures few will be disposed to deny, and applied to Himself frequently where we would least expect such application, convince us that

Christ is in these Psalms much more fully than many are disposed to admit.[15]

The sermons of many of the early church fathers reflect a christocentric understanding of the Psalms. They show Christ speaking either in His own person, individually, or in a broader sense as the Head, praying on behalf of His body, the church. Otherwise, the Psalms are about Christ or are words from the Father to the Son.

### Christ Is Praying These Psalms

Hearing Christ speak in the Psalms gives us the key to these strongly worded curses, and we as people of the Book need this understanding in order to correctly handle the word of truth. One commentator reminds us:

> The circumstance that these Psalms are so unequivocally en-dorsed and appropriated by our blessed Lord . . . will constrain disciples of Christ to touch them with a reverent hand, and rather to distrust their own judgment, than to brand such Scriptures as the products of an unsanctified and unchristian temper.[16]

From our pulpits we who are pastors must firmly maintain that it is only right for the righteous King of Peace to ask God to destroy His enemies. In doing so He affirms the supremacy of God who puts "all enemies under his feet." What a difference it makes in our preaching when we know that these psalms are not the emotional prayers of angry men, but the very war cries of our Prince of Peace!

The Lord Jesus Christ is praying these prayers of vengeance. The prayers that cry out for the utter destruction of the psalmist's enemies can only be grasped when heard from the loving lips of our Lord Jesus. These prayers signal an alarm to all who are still enemies of King Jesus. His prayers will be answered! God's wrath is revealed upon all who oppose Christ. Anyone who rejects God's way of forgiveness in the cross of Christ will bear the dreadful curses of God. He who prays:

> May the table set before them become a snare; may it become
> retribution and a trap. May their eyes be darkened so they cannot
> see, and their backs be bent forever. Pour out your wrath on them;
> let your fierce anger overtake them. May their place be deserted;
> let there be no one to dwell in their tents. For they persecute those
> you wound and talk about the pain of those you hurt. Charge
> them with crime upon crime; do not let them share in your
> salvation. May they be blotted out of the book of life and not be
> listed with the righteous (Ps. 69:23-28),

will one day make this prayer a reality when He says to those on
His left, "Depart from me, you who are cursed, into the eternal
fire prepared for the devil and his angels" (Matt. 25:41).

Professor Fred Leahy of Belfast, Northern Ireland, reminds us
of the vision we need of the imprecatory psalms. Commenting on
Psalm 109 he says:

> But the view which limits Psalm 109 to David and one of his
> adversaries is altogether too short-sighted because it ignores the
> typical nature of David and his kingdom and overlooks the in-
> terpretation of the imprecatory psalms (all of which were written
> by David) in the New Testament, where their ultimate fulfilment
> is seen either in the judgment of Judas or in the apostasy of Israel
> (cf., Rom. 11:9, 10). In the Christian Church Psalm 109 soon be-
> came known as the Psalmus Ischarioticus—the Iscariot Psalm.
> Whether, by rendering the verbs as futures, which may be done,
> the imprecatory psalms be interpreted as predictions rather than
> prayers, makes no moral difference. They remain psalms of
> Christ's holy judgment upon the impenitent in the manner de-
> fined in the New Testament. They belong to His passion and
> crucifixion.[17]

All the enemies of the Lord need to hear these prayers of Christ
proclaimed today. They are not the prayers of a careless and
compassionless tyrant, but the effectual prayers of the Lamb of
God who bore the curse of God for the sins of all who bow their
knee to Him. The wrath of the psalms must be preached as the
wrath of the Lamb of God. God's kingdom is at war!

> I saw heaven standing open and there before me was a white
> horse, whose rider is called Faithful and True. With justice he

judges and makes war. His eyes are like blazing fire, and on his head are many crowns. He has a name written on him that no one but he himself knows. He is dressed in a robe dipped in blood, and his name is the Word of God. The armies of heaven were following him, riding on white horses and dressed in fine linen, white and clean. Out of his mouth comes a sharp sword with which to strike down the nations. "He will rule them with an iron scepter." He treads the winepress of the fury of the wrath of God Almighty (Rev. 19:11-15).

The answer to the question, Who is praying for God to destroy His enemies? is that Jesus Christ is praying. This does not do away with David and the other authors of these psalms but gives fulfillment to their prayers. Jesus is the Messiah—the Anointed King —whose throne and dominion are forever (2 Sam. 7:16; Ps. 89:3, 4).

Our preaching of the Psalms should reflect that David's Lord and greater Son is Jesus Christ. When we understand that it is this merciful and holy Savior of sinners who is praying, we will no longer be ashamed of these prayers, but rather glory in them. Christ's prayers lead us to give God the honor and trust now because we know that God answers His prayers. Therefore, we are assured that the powers of evil will fall and God alone will reign forever!

## Questions for Thought and Discussion

1. How are the Psalms to be understood as God's very own words? (See Rom. 3:2.)

2. How are the Psalms uniquely David's words?

3. Does the Father speak to the Son in the Psalms? Where? (See Heb. 1:5.)

4. How does Christ use the Psalms in the New Testament?

5. How do the apostles use them in preaching Christ?


6. How can the psalms that confess guilt be spoken by Christ?


7. In what sense can all the Psalms be seen as messianic? (See 1 Pet. 1:11.)


### Notes

1. E. W. Hengstenberg, *The Works of Hengstenberg*, vol. 7, *The Psalms* (Cherry Hill, N.J.: Mack, n.d.), p. lxxiii.

2. See Edmund P. Clowney, *The Unfolding Mystery—Discovering Christ in the Old Testament* (Colorado Springs: NavPress, 1988).

3. Quoted by John Peter Lange, *Commentary on the Holy Scriptures*, trans. and ed. Philip Schaff (New York: Charles Scribner's Sons, 1884), p. 4.

4. Dietrich Bonhoeffer, *Psalms: The Prayer Book of the Bible* (Minneapolis: Augsburg, 1970), pp. 18-19.

5. Ibid., p. 20.

6. C. H. Spurgeon, *Commenting and Commentaries* (Grand Rapids: Baker, 1981), pp. 86-87.

7. George Horne, *A Commentary on the Book of Psalms in which their literal and historical sense, as they relate to King David and the people of Israel, is illustrated; and their application to the Messiah, to the church, and to individuals as members thereof* (Philadelphia: Whetham, 1833), p. 28, emphasis added.

8. Ibid., pp. 28-29.

9. Erling C. Olsen, *Meditations in the Book of Psalms* (New York: Loizeaux Brothers, 1939), p. 499.

10. Jonathan Edwards, *Charity and Its Fruits, Christian Love as Manifested in the Heart and Life*, edited from the original manuscripts (London: Banner of Truth, 1969), pp. 178-79, emphasis added.

11. Tremper Longman III, *How to Read the Psalms* (Downers Grove, Ill.: InterVarsity, 1988), pp. 67-68.

12. Andrew Bonar, *Christ and His Church in the Book of Psalms* (Grand Rapids: Kregel, 1978), p. ix.

13. Horne, *Commentary on the Book of Psalms*, p. 19.

14. Ibid., p. 28.

15. J. H. Webster, "The Imprecatory Psalms," in *The Psalms in Worship*, ed. John McNaugher (Pittsburgh: United Presbyterian Board, 1907), p. 307.

16. William Binnie, *The Psalms, Their History, Teachings and Use* (London: Hodder and Stoughton, 1886), p. 278.

17. Frederick S. Leahy, *Satan Cast Out* (Carlisle, Pa: Banner of Truth, 1990), pp. 178-79.

These prayers, then, for woes unutterable upon enemies are the prayers of Christ Himself. But the difficulty to many minds about this is that it seems inconsistent with His prayer for enemies, "Father, forgive them; for they know not what they do." . . . That the two prayers fell from His lips, we know; and that they represent two different things which He received a commission from the Father to do, we know. He has power on earth to forgive sins, and He has power on earth to execute judgment upon enemies. . . . The Psalms themselves present both sides of His Mediatorial character and work in this respect.

James Dick
*Psalm-Singers' Conference*

# 4

# *Are Jesus' Prayers Contradictory?*

Jesus has commanded us to love our enemies (Matt. 5:55). This is an indisputable fact and is a precept that must govern the lives of His followers. As disciples of Christ our obedience is mandatory on this clear issue of loving our personal enemies. There can be no thought of setting aside this often-repeated instruction of our Lord. Its continuing relevance for Christians as long as their earthly warfare shall last was foreseen by A. F. C. Villmar (1800-68) when he said:

> This commandment, that we should love our enemies and forego revenge, will grow even more urgent in the holy struggle which lies before us. . . . The Christians will be hounded from place to place, subjected to physical assault, maltreatment and death of every kind. We are approaching an age of wide-spread persecution. . . . Soon the time will come when we shall pray. . . . It will be a prayer of earnest love for these very sons of perdition who stand around and gaze at us with eyes aflame with hatred and who have perhaps already raised their hands to kill us. . . . Yes, the church which is really waiting for its Lord, and which discerns the signs of the times of decision, must fling itself with its utmost power and with the panoply of its holy life, into this prayer of love.[1]

Jesus' prayer from the cross is a beautiful example of loving prayer in the face of persecution: "Father, forgive them, for they do not know what they are doing." As we seek to understand the war cries of Christ that call for God's vengeance, we must not dilute the force of Jesus' command to love our enemies.

Now you may ask: If it is Jesus' calling for God's vengeance on His enemies in these war psalms, isn't He contradicting His prayer of love for their forgiveness? Is this hopeless double talk?

This question seems to surface in many minds as Christians begin to think through the ramifications of Jesus' speaking in the Psalms. It has been put to me a number of times in seminars that I've given on this subject. Are Jesus' words really contradictory? Let's take a closer look.

In dealing with the area of imprecations or curses in Scriptures, we must address the issue of *apparent* contradictions in the whole of Scripture. We do so not as those who study biblical issues assuming that the Bible is a fallible book containing possible contradictions. They, of course, eagerly search for proofs to support that presupposition. But we have settled that issue and have made a covenant of trust in His Word. And for us who begin with the affirmation that the Bible is the infallible Word of the one true God, seeming contradictions do not undermine our foundation. Instead, we acknowledge the limitation of our understanding and seek by further study to comprehend more clearly the truths revealed for our instruction. In that spirit we shall pursue our task.

### Harmony in the Person of Christ

We must receive Jesus Christ in His fullness if we are to know Him as He really is. He is, of course, the loving and merciful Savior who forgives sin; but He also clearly tells us that He is the one who is coming in judgment on those who disobey His gospel.

We sometimes overlook the *New Testament*'s forceful reminder that

> God is just: He will pay back trouble to those who trouble you and give relief to you who are troubled, and to us as well. This will happen when the Lord Jesus is revealed from heaven in blazing fire with His powerful angels. He will punish those who do not know God and do not obey the gospel of our Lord Jesus.

They will be punished with everlasting destruction and shut out from the presence of the Lord and from the majesty of his power on the day he comes to be glorified in his holy people and to be marveled at among all those who have believed (2 Thess. 1:6-10).

Did you notice how these New Testament words resemble the Psalms? *We have here the very essence and fulfillment of all the imprecatory psalms.* Jesus is indeed the forgiving Savior, and we who have experienced His forgiveness gratefully give Him the praise of our being. But this does not negate that He is also the awesome Judge.

The branches of Christ's church that sing exclusively the Psalms have probably devoted more time than any other people to understanding the Psalms. In 1902 at the Psalm-Singers' Conference in Belfast, Northern Ireland, Professor Dick gave this very lucid explanation to the seeming contradictions of the imprecatory psalms:

These prayers, then, for woes unutterable upon enemies are the prayers of Christ Himself. But the difficulty to many minds about this is that it seems inconsistent with His prayer for enemies, "Father, forgive them; for they know not what they do." There would, indeed be a great inconsistency if Christ had prayed in the same circumstances and concerning the same persons, "Destroy them," and "Forgive them." That the two prayers fell from His lips we know; and that they represent two different things which He received a commission from the Father to do, we know. He has power on earth to forgive sins, and He has power on earth to execute judgment upon enemies. In the one we see His Mediatorial work on one side; in the other we see it on another side. It was fitting that when He was executing His great commission to give His life a ransom for sinners He should offer a prayer that would reveal His goodwill toward men, and would prove incontestably that He was long-suffering, slow to anger, willing to forgive iniquity, transgression, and sin. This, doubtless, and much more that cannot be dwelt on now may be found in the prayer for forgiveness. But there comes a time, and there come circumstances, when His long-suffering has an end, and when those who refuse to kiss the Son must perish from the way when His wrath is kindled but a little. It is equally fitting, then, that in

His Mediatorial character He should pray for their destruction. The Psalms themselves present both sides of His Mediatorial character and work in these respects. "Good and upright is the Lord: therefore will He teach sinners in the way"; "Upon the wicked He shall rain snares, fire and brimstone, and an horrible tempest" (Ps. 25:8; 11:6).[2]

It is interesting that even in the Psalms we see both the vengeance and the love of God and perceive that these two, so often assumed to be enemies, are truly friends in the Person of our Lord Jesus Christ.


*Imprecations in the New Testament*

Let's look with carefulness at the New Testament imprecations of our Lord and Savior. Turning to Matthew 23 we hear Jesus thundering forth "woes" upon the "teachers of the law and Pharisees" whom He unhesitatingly calls "hypocrites." *There follows a seven-fold curse upon their heads!* The seven woes of verses 13, 15, 16, 23, 24, 27, and 29 all condemn and call forth the judgment of God to fall on them in unequivocal terms. Jesus finally says to them: "You snakes! You brood of vipers! How will you escape being condemned to hell?" (v. 33). Do we have an inconsistency in the very ministry of the Savior of love? No, not at all. Rather we have here His loving warning to the wicked to repent. For God's curses will surely overtake forever all unrepentant enemies of Christ.

At another time Jesus takes up Psalm 41:8-10 as a pronouncement of God's vengeance on Judas, the one who betrayed the Lord's Anointed One—the Son of Man. Jesus replied:

> The one who has dipped his hand into the bowl with me will betray me. The Son of Man will go just as it is written about him. But woe to that man who betrays the Son of Man! It would be better for him if he had not been born (Matt. 26:23-24).

We all know the outcome of Judas's traitorous actions. His awful death is described in Acts:

> With the reward he got for his wickedness, Judas bought a field; there he fell headlong, his body burst open and all his intestines spilled out. Everyone in Jerusalem heard about this (1:18-19).

Have you observed the way in which Peter refers two great imprecatory psalms (69 and 109) to Christ's betrayer? Jesus' pronouncement is an echo of the psalms in which Judas' destruction is requested: "Woe to that man who betrays the Son of Man! It would be better for him if he had not been born" (Matt. 26:24). How solemnly does Psalm 41 sound a warning from the now risen and exalted Christ!

> Even my close friend, whom I trusted, he who shared my bread, has lifted up his heel against me. But you, O Lord, have mercy on me (vv. 9-10).

Why?

> "Raise me up, that I may repay them" (v. 10).

If we shrink back from the psalms of God's wrath on the wicked we have not yet understood what took place on the cross! As people cleansed and freed by the transaction that took place there, we must make it our lifelong ambition to grow in knowledge and appreciation of that saving work of God.

If you are a pastor, it is especially crucial for you to apprehend fully that all the curses of God came down upon Christ for us. How else can you rightly expound Paul's teaching: "Christ redeemed us from the curse of the law by becoming a curse for us, for it is written: 'Cursed is everyone who is hung on a tree'" (Gal. 3:13). This is a part of the covenantal curses of Deuteronomy 28.

All who ultimately reject Jesus will suffer the covenantal curse just as certainly as Judas did.

Jesus' prayers of blessing are not for all. On the contrary, His intimate prayer to the Father is carefully recorded in John 17:20-21 for our learning:

> My prayer is . . . for those who will believe in me through their [the apostles'] message, that all of them may be one, Father, just as you are in me and I am in you.

This unity is a covenantal blessing that He does not seek for all mankind. It does not come to those who, like Judas, spurn His way. Our Lord makes this abundantly clear: "I am not praying for the world, but for those you have given me, for they are yours" (v. 9). The Christ who speaks in the Psalms is the same Christ who speaks in the gospels!

### *Paul and the New Testament Curses*
### *(1 Cor. 16:22; Gal. 1:8; 5:12; 2 Tim. 4:14)*

The heart of the apostle Paul is found in his great love for and obedience to Jesus Christ. This love compelled him to urge men to be reconciled to God. His love for his brothers was such that he was moved to exclaim: "For I could wish that I myself were cursed and cut off from Christ for the sake of my brothers" (Rom. 9:3). Yet this same Paul juxtaposes his deep love with the imprecations of the Psalms.

As an apostle of Christ, Paul is a spokesman for Christ, speaking Christ's very words. In this office he writes his letters that, inspired by the Holy Spirit, are given for our instruction. And as an apostle, Paul himself prophesies in imprecatory language. At the conclusion of his first letter to the Corinthians, in fact, where we find one of his strongest utterances, he makes a point of saying, "I, Paul, write this greeting in my own hand." He obviously doesn't want to leave room for any confusion as to the source of this which follows: "If anyone does not love the Lord—a curse be on him. Come, O Lord" (1 Cor. 16:21, 22). What words could be more in harmony with the prayers of the Psalms?

In his epistle to the Galatians we again hear the apostle's heart rise up against all who would preach another gospel. He calls for a curse—an anathema—on them! To have the "anathema" of God is synonymous with being dedicated to eternal destruction. No curse could be worse!

Regarding one who would pervert the gospel of the blessed Lord Jesus, Paul says,

> Let him be eternally condemned! As we have already said, so now I say again: If anybody is preaching to you a gospel other

than what you accepted, let him be eternally condemned! (Gal. 1:8-9).

He is calling out for the damnation of such a one! And he does so not just in passing or in a slip of the tongue, but with strong emphasis and repetition: A curse let him be!

In this same letter Paul expressed a desire to see the agitators against the gospel of free and sovereign grace do themselves physical harm: "As for those agitators, I wish they would go the whole way and emasculate themselves!" (Gal. 5:12). Paul wished that his opponents would not stop with circumcision, but would castrate themselves![3] He didn't mince words, did he? Christ's spokesman understood the theology of the vengeance psalms and prayed in the spirit of the psalms with love for the Lord's cause.

Paul's whole ministry manifests the foundational undergirding of these truths. At the very end of his life he refers to "Alexander the metal worker," who "did me a great deal of harm." Then in keeping both with the Psalms and the ministry of Christ he says, "The Lord will repay him for what he has done" (2 Tim. 4:14). Was this the result of a petty personal dispute with Alexander? No.

Why is he so assured of God's judgment on Alexander? Paul clarifies the issue in his warning to Timothy against this man: "You too should be on your guard against him, because he strongly opposed our message" (v. 15). The spirit of the New Testament is that God's curse rests on all who oppose the good news of Jesus Christ!

### Harmony of the Testaments

God's justice and love form the ground of both Testaments. One day while speaking to a group of local pastors on the imprecatory psalms, I made the point that there has never been a place for *personal* vengeance for God's people. I then quoted Deuteronomy 32:35 (the text, as you may recall, of Jonathan Edwards's great revival sermon, "Sinners in the hands of an angry God"), where the Lord says: "It is mine to avenge; I will repay. In due time their foot will slip; their day of disaster is near and their doom rushes upon them."

One of the pastors challenged the point by asking if this were "really in the New Testament spirit." I directed his attention to Romans 12:19-21 where, to his surprise, we find Paul citing these very words in the context of prohibiting the exercise of *personal* vengeance or evil on anyone in any circumstances.

What is the relationship between God's revenge and ours? Paul answers: "Do not take revenge, my friends, but leave room for God's wrath, for it is written: 'It is mine to avenge; I will repay,' says the Lord" (v. 19). Neither in the Old Testament nor in the New is there a place for personal revenge. All of our vengeance must be given over to the Lord. Every impulse to gratify ourselves by avenging a wrong done to us is surrendered to the Lord as we truly follow Him.

### David's Understanding and Ours

Many have tried to pit the Old and New Testaments against each other, failing to see the whole picture. We have looked at Christ's and His apostles' use and understanding of Old Testament imprecations, and we have seen no contradiction. But what about David? Was he operating under a primitive code of law and wrath, as some insist? Was he expressing personal vindictiveness in his prayers?

David observed the same principles in his time as Paul did later. The Lord's anointed of the Old Testament and the apostle of Christ in the New are in complete friendship. The rule for both is stated well by David, the author of the great majority of the psalms of imprecation. First Samuel 24:12 records his words to his deadly enemy Saul who has been hunting David to kill him (see v. 11):

> May the Lord judge between you and me. And may the Lord avenge the wrongs you have done to me, but my hand will not touch you.

"Vengeance belongs to the Lord" is the rule for all times.

Then where do we get the idea that it is wrong to ask God to bring judgment on the wicked? That mentality creeps up on us so subtly that it has become a very common idea in our day. You may even have heard a fellow Christian express such an intense love for friends or relatives that God's judgment against their evil deeds is rejected. It is possible to perceive such deep feeling of love for another as very "Christian" while failing to realize that what is being expressed actually evidences a *lack of love for God*. In addition, such ideas demonstate a woefully inadequate comprehension of the seriousness of man's sin against a holy God.

Robert L. Dabney, the great Southern Presbyterian theologian of the nineteenth century, hit the nail on the head when he wrote:

> This age has witnessed a whole spawn of religionists, very rife and rampant in some sections of the church, who pretentiously declared themselves the apostles of a lovelier Christianity than that of the sweet Psalmist of Israel. His ethics were entirely too vindictive and barbarous for them, forsooth; and they, with their Peace Societies, and new lights, would teach the world a milder and more beneficent code.[4]

Dabney goes on to speak of Bible expositors who have "fatigued themselves with many vain inventions to explain away the imprecatory language of the Psalms." He relates a distressing instance when Psalm 109 was removed from the Psalter to be replaced by a modern hymn on "the beauty of forgiveness," and he calls us to repentance from the blasphemy of making our unreliable ideals the standard for God:

> All these inventions, then, must be relinquished; the admission must be squarely and honestly made, that the inspired men of both Testaments felt and expressed moral indignation against wrong-doers, and a desire for their proper retribution at the hand of God.[5]

In concluding our observation of the way the prayers of the Psalms dovetail with the entirety of Scripture, I want to challenge your mind with these carefully reasoned thoughts from Dabney:

> Righteous retribution is one of the glories of the divine character. If it is right that God should desire to exercise it, then it cannot be

wrong for his people to desire him to exercise it. It may be objected that, while he claims retribution for himself, he forbids it to them, and that he has thereby forbidden all satisfaction in it to them. The fact is true; the inference does not follow. Inasmuch as retribution inflicted by a creature is forbidden, the desire for its infliction by a creature, or pleasure therein, is also forbidden; but inasmuch as it is righteously inflicted by God, it must be right in him, and must therefore be, when in his hand, a proper subject of satisfaction to the godly.[6]

The various utterances of Christ are *not contradictions but true reflections* of His many shining attributes. In particular, the prayers of the Lord Jesus and of His true followers in both Testaments express His love and His righteous retribution as the holy God who is love personified. This is an essential truth to hold in comprehending the Psalms.

Contradictions? No! On the contrary, we find in the prayers of Jesus the glorious balance and unity of all the attributes of God!

## Questions for Thought and Discussion

1. In what manner can the Christian desire that God exercise retribution?

2. How do the prayers of Christ for judgment reflect God's divine character and will?

3. How can perceiving the wrath of the Lamb be beneficial?

4. What may be implied when one fails to warn of the judgment of the Son?

5. Have we inadvertently weakened our presentation of the gospel message by failing to adequately warn people of God's wrath?

6. What are the intended effects of Jesus' imprecations?

7. How and on whom does Paul use imprecations? Discuss the case of Alexander.

8. Discuss how moral relativism may be responsible for the "Christian" pious attitude of declining to call down God's wrath on the wicked. In what way is it loving to pray these psalms?

9. How has humanism (man's autonomy) influenced the views of many "Christians"?

*Notes*
   1. Quoted by John R. W. Stott, *Christian Counter-Culture* (Downers Grove, Ill.: InterVarsity, 1978), p. 120.
   2. James Dick, "The 'Imprecatory Psalms,'" *Psalm-Singers' Conference* (Belfast: Fountain Printing, 1903), pp. 94-95.
   3. Fritz Rienecker, *A Linguistic Key to the Greek New Testament* (Grand Rapids: Zondervan, 1980), pp. 448-49.
   4. Robert L. Dabney, *Discussions Evangelical and Theological* (London: Banner of Truth, 1967), 1:709-10.
   5. Ibid., p. 711.
   6. Ibid., p. 715.

The church that is conscious of the life and death struggle between the two kingdoms will not exclude hatred for Satan's kingdom from its love for God's kingdom. The church is compelled to show love unto all men and to pray for their conversion. At the same time, with her eye fixed on the promise of the coming day of the Lord in which all God's enemies will be crushed eternally, the church prays for the hastening of the day of judgment.

Harry Mennega
"The Ethical Problem of the Imprecatory Psalms"


God's kingdom cannot come without Satan's kingdom being destroyed. God's will cannot be done in earth without the destruction of evil. Evil cannot be destroyed without the destruction of men who are permanently identified with it. Instead of being influenced by the sickly sentimentalism of the present day, Christian people should realize that the glory of God demands the destruction of evil. Instead of being insistent upon the assumed, but really non-existent, rights of men, they should focus their attention upon the rights of God. Instead of being ashamed of the Imprecatory Psalms, and attempting to apologize for them and explain them away, Christian people should glory in them and not hesitate to use them in the public and private exercises of the worship of God.

Johannes G. Vos
"The Ethical Problem of the Imprecatory Psalms"
*Westminster Theological Journal*

# 5

# May We Pray the Imprecatory Psalms?

## Is There a Need?

Do you use the Psalms as your own prayer book? Are the people to whom you minister learning to pray from the Psalms? Most Christians are in the habit of entering into the spirit of *some* of the Psalms as prayers of their own. Probably every human passion or emotion is expressed in the Psalms. So on any given day a Christian may pick up the Psalms and find a vivid expression of his feelings of the moment, whether discouragement, ecstasy, or simply "hanging in there."

Seeing the Psalms as prayers of the Lord Jesus Christ will deepen your understanding of His heart, His sufferings, and His victory on your behalf. But how do these prayers of Christ become your own personal expressions to God? And how can you who are pastors help the sheep of your flocks to pray the imprecatory psalms?

You may say, "This is the last thing my church needs! If our hearts are lazy and cold to pray for those we *love*, how can we think of praying for *enemies*, as we find in the Psalms?" But I would challenge you, isn't this *the cause* of our lack of prayer? We have not learned from the Lord Jesus how to pray!

Many Christians are like little children who don't ever want to acknowledge being taught anything by another. You will often hear them say, "I know that!" Or, if you ask them where they learned something, they will answer, "I just know it!" as though knowledge began within themselves. Do we have the maturity to recognize that even as Christians we do not pray rightly simply by instinct? The very disciples who were constantly in our Lord's physical presence for instruction felt their need for help in learning to pray. How much more do we need to confess that we are totally unable to pray on our own and humbly ask with those disciples of old, "Lord, teach us to pray"!

The Lord Christ responded by giving them a pattern of prayer in the Lord's Prayer. And when we explore carefully, we find to our amazement that all the praises and petitions of the Psalms fit beautifully under the individual phrases of the Lord's Prayer. In fact, the prayers of Christ in the Psalms can serve as an exposition of the Lord's Prayer, teaching us to pray as Jesus taught His disciples.

The petition, "Your kingdom come, your will be done on earth as it is in heaven," often overlooked as merely introductory, is really pivotal. Here Christ teaches us to pray for the victory of His kingdom. Can we truly utter this prayer without perceiving that our request involves the complete overthrow of Satan's kingdom and all his followers? Martin Luther, that great disciple of Christ in prayer, pointed out that when one prays, "Hallowed be thy name, thy kingdom come, thy will be done," then

> he must put all the opposition to this in one pile and say: "Curses, maledictions and disgrace upon every other name and every other kingdom. May they be ruined and torn apart and may all their schemes and wisdom and plans run aground."[1]

We must be candid enough to acknowledge that to pray for the extension of God's kingdom is to solicit the destruction of all other kingdoms. This is the unique prayer life of the disciples of Christ. When we pray as Jesus taught us, we cry out to God for His blessings upon His church *and for His curses upon the kingdom of the evil one.* As Harry Mennega succinctly stated, "Advance and victory for the Church means retreat and defeat for the kingdom of darkness."[2]

Mennega's excellent unpublished master's thesis gives practical instruction on the prayer life of the Christian:

It is the peculiarly balanced prayer life that the Christian must foster. He is obligated to pray for the conversion of sinners, of those who are now identified with the kingdom of darkness; this he must do in the interest of God's glory. At the same time and in the same interest he must pray for the coming of God's kingdom which involves necessarily praying for the destruction of the kingdom of evil and those who are identified with it. It is in this tension that the Christian must live. Since he does not know who are permanently identified with the kingdom of evil he cannot pray for the doom of known individuals in the way the psalmists did and rather must show love to all people, even his enemies. Yet this prayer for their conversion is accompanied by a prayer for the overthrow of Satan's kingdom, a kingdom which cannot be conceived of apart from its concrete embodiment in actual persons in history.[3]

## Christian Prayer Is Different From Natural Human Emotions

Part of the pastor's work is to equip the saints to do the work of the ministry. Since prayer is a vital component of life and ministry, he must teach God's people how to pray. And what is Christian prayer? It is not just expressing the needs of our heart.

For then we confuse wishes, hopes, sighs, laments, rejoicing—all of which the heart can do by itself—with prayer. Prayer is more than just an expression of emotion. It is finding the way to God and speaking with Him, whether the heart is full or empty. No man can do that by himself. For that he needs Jesus Christ.[4]

When we appropriate the prayers of Jesus Christ we are praying acceptably. Only through His merits are we ever heard by God. Joining Christ, the Head of the church, in praying the Psalms, we make all of our prayers known to God in the name of Jesus. "In Jesus' name" is not to be merely a ritual or a religious formula but the key that opens God's ear for all sinners.

## A Closer Look at Psalm 83

As an example of how to pray a specific psalm of imprecation let us consider Psalm 83. This psalm begins with a vigorous cry for help: "O God, do not keep silent; be not quiet, O God, be not still." Then in verses 2-8 the adversary is recognized as those who "plot together" against God and His people, and the schemes of the wicked are disclosed. In the third section of the psalm we find prayers of vengeance (imprecations) against the enemies of the Lord (vv. 9-15). Finally, in verses 16-18 we are given the sacred purpose of all the prayers of justice: "Cover their faces with shame so that men will seek your name, O Lord. May they ever be ashamed and dismayed; may they perish in disgrace."

How can this become your prayer for today? Well, let me ask, are the forces of evil now fewer in number, power, or boldness than then? On the contrary, the ten enemies named there that set themselves up against God have been multiplied many times over in our day. The whole world has announced its rebellion against God. Even the latest "scientific" technology is being used to mold and promote a godless society.

But we may well wonder, in what manner can God be at-tacked—with atom bombs? *Absurd!* God is truly the exalted One. He sits in the heavens untouched by the puny attacks of men. But the psalmist had noticed the clever way men make their attack upon God: "See how your enemies are astir, how your foes rear their heads. With cunning they conspire against your people; they plot against those you cherish" (vv. 2-3). What form does their assault take? They pounce upon God's people! And that attack is real, just as real as if they were using atom bombs.

Christians today undergo not only physical persecution but daily attempts of the enemy to destroy the church of Jesus Christ from within: temptation to sin, discouragement, and jealousy. We are bombarded on every front. Have you observed that many television commercials are part of an organized onslaught to break down the fortress of the faithful and turn God's people from His way to paths of rebellion against Him? We are constantly prodded to go after what we "deserve." These clever and persua-sive tools instruct us how to "double our pleasure," and even tell us that "weekends were made for Michelob." Evildoers have not changed so much.

"Come," they say, "let us destroy them as a nation, that the name of Israel be remembered no more." With one mind they plot together; they form an alliance against you (vv. 4-5).

The enemies of God are bent on destroying the people of God. This psalm is a prayer for help not just in its original context hundreds of years ago, but for today as well. Its petition is needed as never before by *today's* people of God in their righteous cause.

How does Christ pray? As we read the psalm we find him asking God: *Do to them what you did to others in the past!*

Do to them as you did to Midian, as you did to Sisera and Jabin at the river Kishon, who perished at Endor and became like refuse on the ground (vv. 9-10).

The story of Sisera in the book of Judges provides a painfully vivid example of God's judgment on the wicked. Sisera, as you remember, was a commander in the army of Canaan. "Because he had nine hundred iron chariots and had cruelly oppressed the Israelites for twenty years, they cried to the Lord for help" (Judg. 4:3). God's response to that cry for help is given in the following verses:

The Lord routed Sisera and all his chariots and army by the sword, and Sisera abandoned his chariot and fled on foot. . . . All the troops of Sisera fell by the sword; not a man was left (vv. 15-16).

The account goes on to describe with deliberate detail how Sisera then escaped to the tent of Jael, the wife of Heber the Kenite, where he was warmly welcomed:

"Come, my lord, come right in. Don't be afraid." So he entered her tent, and she put a covering over him. "I'm thirsty," he said. "Please give me some water." She opened a skin of milk, gave him a drink, and covered him up. "Stand in the doorway of the tent," he told her. "If someone comes by and asks you, 'Is anyone here?' say 'No.'" But Jael, Heber's wife, picked up a tent peg and a hammer and went quietly to him while he lay fast asleep, exhausted. She drove the peg through his temple into the ground, and he died (Judg. 4:18-21).

Are we to pray that God will do *this* to our personal enemies: "O God, pound a tent peg into their head!"? Listen carefully to the words of Deborah and Barak's song celebrating the victory:

> He asked for water, and she gave him milk; in a bowl fit for nobles she brought him curdled milk. Her hand reached for the tent peg, her right hand for the workman's hammer. She struck Sisera, she crushed his head, she shattered and pierced his temple. At her feet he sank, he fell; there he lay. At her feet he sank, he fell; where he sank, there he fell—dead (Judg. 5:25-27).

So, do we say: "Do it again, Lord! Do that to my own enemy!"? *Never!* Never may God's people pray so out of a spirit of personal vengeance against their enemies. Do we need to be reminded again of our Commander's orders to love even our enemies?

Without assistance how can we ever righteously pray this prayer? I answer this question unequivocally: *We never can!* We cannot pray this prayer on our own . . . not because we are too *good*, but rather because we are too prone to evil! Yet we must *learn* to pray it. How?

*First, We Must Learn to Pray in Christ*

If we cannot offer *any* prayer apart from Jesus Christ, how much less this prayer of God's wrath and vengeance! As we abide in Christ we learn what it is to pray, "not my will but thine be done." We request not our own *personal* advancement or victory over our private enemies but rather the advancement of *His* kingdom—that His enemies be destroyed. When the enemies of God attack us, we deliberately lay down the sword of personal revenge. If we attempt to avenge ourselves we are still seeking our own way, taking things into our own hands.

To pray the imprecations of the Psalms is to surrender all rights for vengeance to God. It means being prepared to suffer and to endure without personal revenge or hatred as Christ did. It involves being gentle and loving even when I am reviled and persecuted. It encompasses acknowledging in all my ways that God's cause is more important than I am.

In fact, to understand fully the imprecations in the Psalms it is essential to remember that "the welfare of man is not the chief end of man" (not even the welfare of redeemed man). Do not forget "that we sinful creatures have no inherent rights which our holy Maker must respect" (not even rights to pursue our own defense).

> God may, without violating any obligation, take any man's life at any time and in any way; and that it is one with this for God to inspire the Psalmist to pray that he should do so in a particular instance, the prayer itself being altogether proper since it is divinely inspired.[5]

We must learn to pray Christ's imprecations just as He taught us to pray, "Thy kingdom come, thy will be done." Only *in Christ* can we truly make these prayers for *Christian* victory.

### Second, God's Word Is the Foundation

The psalmist is pleading, As you have faithfully destroyed the wicked in the past, do so now. This is the essence of his request: "May all who have set themselves against you be destroyed." We have observed that such a prayer may not be made because of personal hatred or revenge. *Never!*

But there was an earlier scriptural principle and precedent that guided even the psalmist's attitude. Hundreds of years before the Psalms were written God had said through His prophet Moses:

> If you do not carefully follow all the words of this law, which are written in this book, and do not revere this glorious and awesome name—the Lord your God—the Lord will send fearful plagues on you and your descendants, harsh and prolonged disasters, and severe and lingering illnesses. He will bring upon you all the diseases of Egypt that you dreaded, and they will cling to you. The Lord will also bring on you every kind of sickness and disaster not recorded in this Book of the Law until you are destroyed. You who were as numerous as the stars in the sky will be left but few in number, because you did not obey the Lord your God. Just as it pleased the Lord to make you prosper and increase in number, so it will please him to ruin and destroy you. You will

be uprooted from the land you are entering to possess (Deut. 28: 58-63).

The covenant God made with His people included curses for disobedience as well as blessings for obedience. Deuteronomy 27 records the formal giving and receiving of the covenant terms in an awesome account:

> The Levites shall recite to all the people of Israel in a loud voice:
> "Cursed is the man who carves an image or casts an idol—a thing detestable to the Lord, the work of the craftsman's hands—and sets it up in secret." Then all the people shall say, "Amen!"
> "Cursed is the man who dishonors his father or his mother." Then all the people shall say, "Amen!"
> "Cursed is the man who moves his neighbor's boundary stone." Then all the people shall say, "Amen!"
> "Cursed is the man who leads the blind astray on the road." Then all the people shall say, "Amen!"
> "Cursed is the man who withholds justice from the alien, the fatherless or the widow." Then all the people shall say, "Amen!"
> "Cursed is the man who sleeps with his father's wife, for he dishonors his father's bed." Then all the people shall say, "Amen!"
> "Cursed is the man who has sexual relations with any animal." Then all the people shall say, "Amen!"
> "Cursed is the man who sleeps with his sister, the daughter of his father or the daughter of his mother." Then all the people shall say, "Amen!"
> "Cursed is the man who sleeps with his mother-in-law." Then all the people shall say, "Amen!"
> "Cursed is the man who kills his neighbor secretly." Then all the people shall say, "Amen!"
> "Cursed is the man who accepts a bribe to kill an innocent person." Then all the people shall say, "Amen!"
> "Cursed is the man who does not uphold the words of this law by carrying them out." Then all the people shall say, "Amen!" (vv. 14-26).

Do you see how important it is to grasp the significance of the Old Testament foundations we have been given? If God pronounced a curse even upon His own covenant people, how much more will He destroy the ungodly who rebel against Him? Men set up their own kingdoms, but God has set up His King upon His holy hill, and of those who dare to defy Him, we are told, He "will dash them to pieces like pottery" (Ps. 2:9).

Do you pray that this curse may come upon the enemies of God today? Do you ask God to destroy His enemies today as He has in the past? Do you who are pastors instruct your people in this kind of prayer? Surely you *must* if you pray in line with God's Word and His promises for the future. Isn't this the very essence of New Testament prophecies?

Does any passage in the entire Old Testament tell more powerfully of God's paying back "trouble" to those who trouble the people of God than these covenant curses? And once again we find the New Testament echoing the same spirit when it says in 2 Thessalonians:

> God is just: He will pay back trouble to those who trouble you and give relief to you who are troubled, and to us as well. This will happen when the Lord Jesus is revealed from heaven in blazing fire with his powerful angels. He will punish those who do not know God and do not obey the gospel of our Lord Jesus. They will be punished with everlasting destruction and shut out from the presence of the Lord and from the majesty of his power on the day he comes to be glorified in his holy people and to be marveled at among all those who have believed. This includes you, because you believed our testimony to you (1:6-10).

We must pray these psalms based on God's prophetic Word of "everlasting destruction." The issue at hand is not, Does this psalm express my desires of this moment? but rather, Is my desire truly, "Thy kingdom come, Thy will be done"?

### Third, Conversion Is the Goal of Our Prayer

In verse 16 of the psalm we are given one of the reasons that we should desire that the enemy be brought down. As we pray with the psalmist, "Cover their faces with shame," do we again wonder, "Why?" It is not out of personal hatred or the spirit of a vendetta. Neither is it so that we can gloat over their destruction.

Of course not! Our prayer must be, with the psalmist, "so that men will seek your name, O Lord." *Why* are we taught to pray for God's judgment on the enemy? *So that they will be converted!* Nothing could be clearer from this prayer.

"Wait a minute!" says the modern scholar. "I can't accept that!" Mitchell Dahood, recognized Ugaritic scholar of the *Anchor Bible*, for instance, argues that to pray for the conversion of the enemy in this way "is hardly amenable to coherent exegesis within the immediate context and does not accord with the pervading spirit of this Psalm."[6] Then this particular scholar proposes to solve the dilemma he created by changing the text of Scripture! But we are handling God's own Word, given with purpose. God is revealing to us a primary reason to utter these powerful prayers *in Jesus Christ*: we pray so that by means of God's judgment they will be *converted.*

Isn't the same principle repeatedly at work in Scripture? How often do we see God's judgment leading men to repentance! Look at the example of Saul of Tarsus, the great persecutor of the early church, who in his rebellion against Christ was brought to blindness on the road to Damascus. He was granted repentance, faith, and much understanding. Later as the inspired apostle, Paul adds to the clear New Testament witness on this issue:

> Now we know that God's judgment against those who do such things is based on truth. So when you, a mere man, pass judgment on them and yet do the same things, do you think you will escape God's judgment? Or do you show contempt for the riches of his kindness, tolerance and patience, not realizing that God's kindness leads you toward repentance? (Rom. 2:2-4).

*God consistently leads men to Himself through judgment.* There are certain conclusions we can draw from this truth that will help us pray with understanding.

*1. No affliction or judgment is too great if it causes us to seek the Lord!*
Verse 13 pleads, "Make them like tumbleweed," that is, rootless and homeless, blown about by the wind. This would be but the kindness of God if it causes men to seek the Lord. Ask King Nebuchadnezzar if his becoming temporarily like an ox did not

result in great blessing. Hear him finally seeking and praising God after seven years of judgment:

> At the end of that time, I, Nebuchadnezzar, raised my eyes toward heaven, and my sanity was restored. Then I praised the Most High; I honored and glorified him who lives forever. His dominion is an eternal dominion; his kingdom endures from generation to generation. All the peoples of the earth are regarded as nothing. He does as he pleases with the powers of heaven and the peoples of the earth. No one can hold back his hand or say to him: "What have you done?" (Dan. 4:34-35).

David Dickson, a Puritan commentator on the Psalms, had it right when he wrote,

> If any of the enemies of God's people belong to God's election, the Church's prayer against them giveth way to their conversion, and seeketh no more than that the judgment should follow them, only until they acknowledge their sin, turn, and seek God.[7]

Verses 14-15 picture a raging forest fire that completely routs the enemy from its land. How can this result in conversions? The land of Afghanistan gives us a sobering present-day example of this judgment. Afghanistan has been closed to the gospel with very few Christians in the entire country for many years. As a people they have rejected God's good news, and consequently they have experienced harsh judgment in many forms. But the dreaded invasion of the Soviet troops caused many Afghans to flee to refugee camps outside the borders of their country. In the turmoil and constant change of these camps many Afghans have come to seek the Lord. Some of these are now returning to their homeland as new creatures in Christ, taking the good news of Jesus Christ to their own people. They were covered with shame so that they would seek the Lord.

No judgment is too great if it drives people to seek the true God in Jesus Christ. We must learn to pray with this understanding for evil men today. Yes, we ardently desire that they will be led by God's judgment to repentance and faith in Jesus Christ and be saved—even the worst of enemies!

2. *All will experience either conversion or final judgment.* "But what if they don't ever seek the Lord?" you may ask. We must desire with the same intensity that if they continue in rebellion they will incur God's final judgment.[8]

Luther's exposition of John 17:9 gives us careful instruction and a true illustration of this prayer for our enemies:

> We should pray that our enemies be converted and become our friends, and if not, that their doing and designing be bound to fail and have no success and that their persons perish rather than the Gospel and the kingdom of Christ. Thus the saintly martyr Anastasia, a wealthy, noble Roman matron, prayed against her husband, an idolatrous and terrible ravager of Christians, who had flung her into a horrible prison, in which she had to stay and die. There she lay and wrote to the saintly Chrysogonus diligently to pray for her husband that, if possible, he be converted and believe; but if not, that he be unable to carry out his plans and that he soon make an end of his ravaging. Thus she prayed him to death, for he went to war and did not return home. So we, too, pray for our angry enemies, not that God protect and strengthen them in their ways, as we pray for Christians, or that He help them, but that they be converted, if they can be; or, if they refuse, that God oppose them, stop them and end the game to their harm and misfortune.[9]

3. *Here is hope for revival!* Could it be that God may bring revival to many lands through judgment? God's judgment has caused the most godless of people to seek the Lord. Wasn't this Habakkuk's prayer? After knowing of God's judgment he cried out: "Lord, I have heard of your fame; I stand in awe of your deeds, O Lord. Renew them in our day, in our time make them known; in wrath remember mercy" (Hab. 3:2; see Ps. 11:6; Prov. 25:22; Rom. 12:20).

4. *The end purpose of all our prayer is that God may be glorified.* God's glory stands sublime and towers over all of creation. That Jehovah has made everything for "his own purpose" is a fundamental truth of both Testaments. Proverbs 16:4 clearly states that even the wicked were created for the day of evil. God's glory is truly the greatest good.

## Needed Today: A Revolution in Prayer

The revolution that Copernicus spearheaded in the realm of cosmology challenged a worldwide misconception of his time. His research proved the radical notion that the true center of the solar system was not the earth but the sun. In his classic work, *Revolution of the Celestial Orbs*, Copernicus showed that the prevailing conception of the cosmos needed drastic change.

In a similar way today we need to challenge Christendom which has itself as the prime focus of existence. Can we not recognize the error of having our prayers revolve around our feelings, wants, and comforts? Have our prayers become so man-centered that we actually cringe to utter prayers that have God's glory as their final end? This is indeed the fearful condition of the church today. *We need a Copernican revolution in our prayers!* What a difference we would see if the church began to perceive that God's absolute glory is truly the center. May the centrality of God, and God alone, be the goal of our learning!

Let this be the prayer of our hearts: "O Christ, come in power and show forth the glory of God. Bring judgment to the wicked that they may seek you . . . and if not, O God, destroy all who won't bow to you. Let them know that only you, whose name is the Lord, are the Most High over all the earth."

Lord, teach us to pray: "If anyone does not love the Lord, a curse be on him. Come, O Lord!" (1 Cor. 16:22).

## Questions for Thought and Discussion

1. Read and study the Psalms with the petitions of the Lord's Prayer in mind and note how they correspond.

2. Show how a balanced presentation of God's love and God's wrath will lead men to know that He alone is the Most High over all the earth. (See Ps. 83:18b.)

3. What grand end is in view in the prayers of vengeance?

4. How should the Christian *not* use these psalms?

5. How do the prayers of imprecation enable the Christian to endure and triumph over persecution?

6. Note the correlation between Old Testament promises of judgment and those in the New, especially as recorded in Hebrews 2:1-3; 3:1-4:12; 10:26-31; 12:22-28.

7. Why do we need to pray all the prayers the Bible teaches? (Can our conscience be a sufficient or autonomous guide to prayer?)

8. Should we always pray for peace, plenty, and prosperity?

9. Discuss and be aware of the revolutionary difference between man-centered and God-centered prayer.

**Notes**

1. Martin Luther, *Luther's Works*, ed. Jaroslav Pelikan (St. Louis: Concordia, 1956), 21:101.

2. Harry Mennega, "The Ethical Problem of the Imprecatory Psalms" (master's thesis, Westminster Theological Seminary, 1959), p. 93.

3. Ibid.

4. Dietrich Bonhoeffer, *Psalms: The Prayer Book of the Bible* (Minneapolis, Augsburg, 1970), p. 10.

5. Meredith G. Kline, *The Structure of Biblical Authority* (Grand Rapids: Eerdmans, 1972), p. 161.

6. Mitchell Dahood, *The Anchor Bible*, vol. 17, *Psalms II* (Garden City, N.Y.: Doubleday, 1968), p. 277.

7. David Dickson, *Commentary on the Psalms* (Minneapolis: Klock and Klock, 1980), 2:67.

8. See John Stott, *Christian Counter-Culture* (Downers Grove, Ill.: InterVarsity, 1978), p. 117.

9. Martin Luther, *What Luther Says* (St. Louis: Concordia, 1959), p. 1100.

When Jesus Christ sent seventy-two disciples on a preaching mission, He told them to proclaim the coming of God's Kingdom (Lk. 10:9)—that is, to announce that people must submit to God's rule in their lives. Jesus instructed them to pray for peace on any house they approached, assuring them that those who welcomed the message would have peace, but that if anyone rejected it, the peace would return on the disciples (verse 5). But we must consider what He said they should do if their message were rejected—that is, if the hearers persisted in rebellion against God's rule—"But when you enter a town and are not welcomed, go into its streets and say, 'Even the dust of your town that sticks to our feet we wipe off against you. Yet be sure of this: The kingdom of God is near'" (verses 10-11).

What would be the result of that denunciation? I tell you, it will be more bearable on that day for Sodom [on which God sent fire from Heaven in judgment for its wickedness] than for that town (verse 12). Immediately Jesus added curses on Korazin, Bethsaida, and Capernaum for their rejection of His message (verses 13-15). He then explained to the disciples the great authority He had given them: "He who listens to you listens to me; he who rejects you rejects me; but he who rejects me rejects him who sent me" (verse 16). This is the fundamental basis for calling down God's curses on anyone: his persistent rebellion against God's authority expressed in His Law and the ministry of His servants.

E. Calvin Beisner
*Psalms of Promise*

# 6

# *How Can We Preach These Prayers?*

The church of Jesus Christ is an army under orders. Scripture constitutes the official dispatch from the Commander-in-Chief. But we have a problem: those who are called to pass on those orders to others are refusing to do so. How then can we expect to be a united, effective army? Is it any wonder that the troops have lost sight of their commission to demolish the strongholds of the kingdom of darkness? If the church does not hear the battle cries of her Captain, how will she follow Him onto the battlefield?

Pastors are commissioned to pass on the orders of the church's Commander, never withholding or changing His words. One whose job is to carry dispatches to troops in wartime would face certain and severe punishment if he dared to amend the general's orders. The pastor's charge is of greater importance than that of a courier in any earthly army. There's no place for this dispatcher to second-guess his orders or decide he doesn't agree with his Commander's strategy.

We have seen that the Psalms are much more than devotional words written in green pastures long ago. Ministers of the gospel must now follow through and communicate their message to the troops.

Understanding and praying the Psalms is important, but if we stop there we fail to carry out God's commission. It is time to announce the war cries from the Psalms clearly and forcefully. Only then will the church of Jesus Christ awake from lethargy and rise once again to battle. A lack of urgency in the soldiers and confusion in the ranks should not surprise us if we have failed to pass on the battle cry.

I have searched extensively for a manual of helpful instruction for pastors in preaching the imprecatory psalms and have found none. I pray that this chapter will be used of God to give increased understanding and assistance in this task.

In accepting the challenge of preaching these psalms, there are three biblical motifs we pastors must investigate and communicate: *(1) the covenantal context of the psalm:* Where does it fit into the big picture of the history of God's promises to His people?; *(2) the christological context of the psalm:* What light does the new covenant of Jesus Christ shed on this psalm?; and *(3) the cultural context of the psalm:* How does this psalm apply to us in today's world?

## *The Covenantal Context of the Psalms*

The Psalms, like the rest of Scripture, must be understood and preached from their covenantal context. Long ago God established a relationship with fallen man by means of a covenant. In dealing with His covenant people, God clearly set forth covenantal blessings for those who keep His covenant and covenantal curses for those who break it.

You may ask how this pertains to the Psalms. Did you ever notice that even the very first psalm, so simple yet profound, is firmly set in the framework of that covenant? God promises blessing to him who "does not walk in the counsel of the wicked or stand in the way of sinners or sit in the seat of mockers" (v. 1). The psalmist also reminds us that "the way of the wicked will perish" (v. 6). So at the very beginning of the prayer book, the principles of the historic covenant are laid out as the basis of God's way with men.

Deuteronomy 26-30 gives us a summary of God's covenant blessings and curses. Notice that the blessings were accompanied by commands:

> The Lord your God commands you this day to follow these decrees and laws; carefully observe them with all your heart and

with all your soul. You have declared this day that the Lord is your God and that you will walk in his ways, that you will keep his decrees, commands and laws, and that you will obey him. And the Lord has declared this day that you are his people, his treasured possession as he promised, and that you are to keep all his commands. He has declared that he will set you in praise, fame and honor high above all the nations he has made and that you will be a people holy to the Lord your God, as he promised (26:16-19).

Chapter 27 tells how the Levites recited in a loud voice to all the people of God the *curses* for covenant breakers. Read these curses and think how the psalmist prays in the context of these curses. Chapter 28 follows with promises of abundant *blessings* for covenant keepers:

If you fully obey the Lord your God and carefully follow all his commands I give you today, the Lord your God will set you high above all the nations on earth. All these blessings will come upon you and accompany you if you obey the Lord your God: You will be blessed in the city and blessed in the country. The fruit of your womb will be blessed, and the crops of your land and the young of your livestock—the calves of your herds and the lambs of your flocks. Your basket and your kneading trough will be blessed. You will be blessed when you come in and blessed when you go out (vv. 1-6).

The life of the "blessed man" of Psalm 1 can be fully realized only in Christ. He is the only one who *never* "walks in the counsel of the wicked or stands in the way of sinners or sits in the seat of mockers." Only of Him can it be truly said that "whatever he does prospers." The Lord's anointed who writes the Psalms prays consciously in the context of the covenant. This is exactly what we have in the prayers of blessing in the Psalms. God will prosper those who obey Him.

In Deuteronomy we see that the curses for covenant breakers are also numerous:

However, if you do not obey the Lord your God and do not carefully follow all his commands and decrees I am giving you today, all these curses will come upon you and overtake you: You will be cursed in the city and cursed in the country. Your basket and your kneading trough will be cursed. The fruit of your womb will be cursed, and the crops of your land, and the calves of your herds and the lambs of your flocks. You will be cursed when you come in and cursed when you go out. The Lord will send on you curses, confusion and rebuke in everything you put your hand to, until you are destroyed and come to sudden ruin because of the evil you have done in forsaking him (28:15-20).

What comprehensive curses! The passage goes on to say:

The Lord will plague you with diseases until he has destroyed you from the land you are entering to possess. The Lord will strike you with wasting disease, with fever and inflammation, with scorching heat and drought, with blight and mildew, which will plague you until you perish. The sky over your head will be bronze, the ground beneath you iron. The Lord will turn the rain of your country into dust and powder; it will come down from the skies until you are ruined. The Lord will cause you to be defeated before your enemies. You will come at them from one direction but flee from them in seven, and you will become a thing of horror to all the kingdoms on earth. Your carcasses will be food for all the birds of the air and the beasts of the earth, and there will be no one to frighten them away. The Lord will afflict you with the boils of Egypt and with tumors, festering sores and the itch, from which you cannot be cured. The Lord will afflict you with madness, blindness and confusion of mind. At midday you will grope about like a blind man in the dark. You will be unsuccessful in everything you do; day after day you will be oppressed and robbed, with no one to rescue you (28:21-29).

How often do we read these words and let our minds absorb their solemnity?

These are the very curses that the psalmist invokes upon the enemies of the Lord's Anointed in his day. Remember, he is not praying for his personal cause, but rather that *God's* cause would prevail by the carrying out of His covenant promises. It is evident from his plea in Psalm 109 that the psalmist has this acute curse upon the "fruit of the womb" of covenant breakers in mind:

> May his children be fatherless and his wife a widow. May his children be wandering beggars; may they be driven from their ruined homes (vv. 9, 10).

In verses 13-15 he goes on to say:

> May his descendants be cut off, their names blotted out from the next generation.... May their sins always remain before the Lord, that he may cut off the memory of them from the earth.

It is essential as we study any psalm that we take into consideration the same facts the psalmist had in view.

The closing chapters of Deuteronomy list even more curses, which, again, so closely parallel the prayers of the psalmist. (See Deut. 32:19-35, for example.)

It makes a tremendous impact on God's people when they see the war psalms as prayers for God to do what He promised in His covenant long ago. The eternal truth is that God cannot be mocked; a man reaps what he sows (Gal. 6:7). All of Scripture agrees and proclaims that the covenantal *curses* are as real as the blessings. How can this covenantal concept be taught from the pulpit?

*First,* since in our day this covenantal framework has been either forgotten or rejected as inferior religion, *it is essential to explain it fully and stress it repeatedly.* It may be necessary initially for you to make an in-depth study of the covenant before you can give foundational instruction to others.

Have you recognized that the words from Deuteronomy 28:26, which prophesy, "Your carcasses will be food for all the birds of the air and the beasts of the earth, and there will be no one to frighten them away," refers to the cutting of the covenant in Genesis 15? On that memorable occasion God set the terms of the covenant and then passed between the halves of the animals of sacrifice, thereby pledging Himself in covenant faithfulness. Geerhardus Vos, in one of his many penetrating exegetical comments on the covenant, states:

> There is probably no case surpassing this in anthropomorphic realism within the Old Testament. The dividing of the animals and the walking of God (alone) between the pieces literally sig-

nified that God invokes upon Himself the fate of dismemberment in case He should not keep faith with Abraham (cpr. Jer. 34:18-19).[1]

The curses of the covenant are said to rest on all who violate the covenant—even God Himself and His Anointed One—should they be unfaithful. Also in covenantal context the psalmist prays for God to mete out judgment upon himself if he has been guilty. Listen to his words in Psalm 7:

> O Lord my God, if I have done this and there is guilt on my hands—if I have done evil to him who is at peace with me or without cause have robbed my foe—then let my enemy pursue and overtake me; let him trample my life to the ground and make me sleep in the dust (vv. 3-5).

These pertinent facts should whet your appetite for a deeper investigation of the covenant in relation to the Psalms.[2] Too many Christians in our churches do not have a clue about the far-reaching significance of the covenant.

*Second, we must show how God has fulfilled His covenant in history*—not just in biblical history but in world history as well. Let me illustrate. Look how completely God has fulfilled His Word in relation to the Jewish nation. God said through Moses:

> Because you did not serve the Lord your God joyfully and gladly in the time of prosperity, therefore in hunger and thirst, in nakedness and dire poverty, you will serve the enemies the Lord sends against you. He will put an iron yoke on your neck until he has destroyed you. The Lord will bring a nation against you from far away, from the ends of the earth, like an eagle swooping down, a nation whose language you will not understand, a fierce-looking nation without respect for the old or pity for the young. They will devour the young of your livestock and the crops of your land until you are destroyed. They will leave you no grain, new wine or oil, nor any calves of your herds or lambs of your flocks until you are ruined. They will lay siege to all the cities throughout your land until the high fortified walls in which you trust fall down. They will besiege all the cities throughout the land the Lord your God is giving you. Because of the suffering that your enemy will inflict on you during the siege, you will eat the fruit

of the womb, the flesh of the sons and daughters the Lord your God has given you (Deut. 28:47-53).

These frightful words were not empty threats. They *were fulfilled* in Samaria (see 2 Kings 6:28-29) and then again in Judea when the Roman army destroyed Jerusalem in A.D. 70. Josephus says,

> The Roman armies at length besieged, sacked, and utterly desolated Jerusalem; and during the siege, the famine was so extreme that even rich and delicate persons, both men and women, ate their own children.[3]

The preaching of the Psalms must focus people's attention on God's curses and show His hand at work in history. God's wrath on covenant breakers is real!

If you have been among the many Christians who use the Psalms as simply sweet devotional experiences, I hope that your own grasp and subsequent communication of the Psalms will begin to reflect a covenantal understanding. Edmund Clowney speaks the truth when he says that the Psalms are

> memorial utterance . . . not just private meditations. . . . They are not pages from the diary of an individual that happen to have been preserved for their beauty. They are the utterances of those who stand before God in the structure of the covenant and who are memorializing God's faithfulness.[4]

We pastors must examine and expound each psalm in the light of the sacred covenant God cut in the presence of Abram so long ago. That context is a bright sun whose far-reaching beams illuminate the imprecatory psalms.

### The Christological Context of the Psalms

We have seen the importance of the covenantal context, from *beforehand*, in which the Psalms were set. Now it is fitting to develop the fact that *after* the Psalms were prayed, more was added to Scripture that gives further enlightenment on their interpretation. We who have the New Testament can never look at the Old as if the New did not exist. Rather, we have the privilege of looking back in time through the eyes of New Testament writers to the christological context of the Psalms. David's greater Son, Christ Himself, was in David even then, offering the prayers of the Psalms.

We have observed that the "I" of the Psalms is Jesus Christ. The "we" of the Psalms includes us as we are in the Lord Jesus, who prays with His people to the loving Father. The enemies are not our own, individually, but those of the Lord's Christ and of His church. So it is not enough for you to know the temporal context of each psalm and explain its historical setting. That would be to understand the Psalms in merely a Jewish way. They are the Psalms of Christ as Prophet, Priest, and King. They record Christ's march in victory against the kingdom of darkness.

As Christ is the author of the Psalms, so, too, is He the final fulfillment of the covenant on which they are based. God will answer the psalmist's prayers completely in Jesus Christ on the final day of judgment. While on earth Jesus foretold the day when He will say: "But those enemies of mine who did not want me to be king over them—bring them here and kill them in front of me" (Luke 19:27). Norval Geldenhuys, writing in the *New International Commentary*, points out the correlation of this passage with past and future events:

> A fatal end awaits everyone who refuses to acknowledge and to obey Jesus as King and Lord. In the disasters that befell the Jewish people (especially during the Roman-Jewish war of A.D. 66-70 when Jerusalem was completely destroyed and hundreds of thousands of Jews were killed), these words have already found fulfillment. At the second advent of Jesus, however, they will be completely and finally fulfilled when all who have rejected Him will reap the retribution of everlasting loss.[5]

How important it is to warn people of the implications of these prayers! We will fail as messengers if we preach the Psalms of David only as high points of a devotional diary. We must lift up Christ and show the glorious truth that He is *central* in the Psalms.

I have provided in an appendix a list of the New Testament uses of the Psalms to assist pastors in preaching each psalm in its christological context. To preach these psalms biblically you must first understand their relationship to Jesus Christ, the living Word. The riches of Jesus Christ must be our theme from the Psalms—not the poverty of the hearts of men or our own needs.

Here is a practical suggestion in carrying out this commission: seek to answer the questions, How does the *New Testament* interpret this psalm of imprecation we have before us? and How is *Christ speaking* in this psalm according to the New Testament pattern? I recognize that this will demand intense study. But I can tell you from personal experience, it is well worth the effort!

I had the privilege of preaching from Psalm 137 in Sao Paulo, Brazil, in October, 1988. People who had never understood this psalm were suddenly full of interest because they saw Christ at work in the destruction of Babylon and the children of darkness. A few months earlier I had preached from this famous imprecatory psalm in inner-city Philadelphia. After the service I was surrounded by people asking questions about Christ's final victory over the kingdom of Satan. God's people want to know how the New Testament interprets the Psalms.

I've included in the appendices two messages in summary form on Psalms 58 and 137 to show how our sermons can answer these questions and proclaim Christ as Lord of the Psalms.

If you are a pastor, accept the challenge to preach Christ from the Psalms. God's people will be blessed by their enlarged vision of Him. This christological context is essential for New Testament preaching of the Psalms.

### The Cultural Context of the Psalms

In expounding the Psalms, we must give due attention to their historical setting. Some of them provide clues either in the text itself or in the superscriptions, which are ancient and reliable. This cultural background is necessary in order to grasp the historical relevancy of any given psalm.

Make every effort to comprehend each psalm as the generation that first sang it did. This will involve studying the psalm in the original language, making a literary analysis, and examining Old Testament historical relationships. The importance of this historical concept becomes apparent as you recognize the witness it gives to God's great work of redemption. The search for the setting must not cause us, however, to overlook the most essential element of any psalm: the message of God for His people today.

As you study the literary classification, the exact date of the psalm, the historical characters involved, and the surrounding Old Testament events of the psalm, you will find that it illuminates God's work of redemption in Christ.

A sermon without the saving Christ *for our culture* is no sermon at all! All the pertinent facts of a given psalm must be directed so that they bring into focus the message of Christ.

Through the study of the cultural context of the psalm in David's time we uncover its relevance for our own culture. The Psalms' application to Christians today does not rest on the cleverness of the preacher's imagination. Rather, in each psalm the eternal Christ Himself speaks to the hearts of His people now.

## Applying the Psalms From Their Culture to Ours

### The Christian Warfare

Hearing expositions of these war psalms of the Prince of Peace will remind His people that God's kingdom is at war! The kingdom of darkness is being overcome by the kingdom of Jesus Christ, a war in which each local congregation of believers plays a vital part. You must rally your battalion to put on the whole armor of God, including "the sword of the Spirit, which is the Word of God" (Eph. 6:17). That battle-readiness also involves "pray[ing] in the Spirit on all occasions with all kinds of prayers and requests" (Eph. 6:18).

Christ teaches His army to pray for the utter destruction of the enemies of God as the psalmist did: "Pour out your wrath on the nations that do not acknowledge you, on the kingdoms that do not call on your name" (Ps. 79:6). Isn't this how Paul, too, prayed in the Christian warfare: "If anyone does not love the Lord—a curse be on him. Come, O Lord!" (1 Cor. 16:22)?

These psalms must be preached in such a way that the soldiers recognize they are in a war far more serious than any war David or the armies of Israel ever fought! David's time is long past, but the battle continues. God's army in every place needs the war psalms of her Prince of Peace. The Christian church has lost its military vision because the pulpit has been ashamed of the battle cries from the Psalms.

## Traitors and Deserters Must Be Warned

A number of imprecations call for God's justice to fall upon the unfaithful "friend." For instance, Psalm 55 says,

> If an enemy were insulting me, I could endure it; if a foe were raising himself against me, I could hide from him. But it is you, a man like myself, my companion, my close friend, with whom I once enjoyed sweet fellowship as we walked with the throng at the house of God. . . . My companion attacks his friends; he violates his covenant. His speech is smooth as butter, yet war is in his heart; his words are more soothing than oil, yet they are drawn swords (vv. 12-14, 20-21).

In the same psalm God calls for the apostate's destruction:

> Let death take my enemies by surprise; let them go down alive to the grave, for evil finds lodging among them. . . . But you, O God, will bring down the wicked into the pit of corruption; blood-thirsty and deceitful men will not live out half their days (vv. 15, 23).

This warning applies today to those who appear among God's people but do not bear the fruit of righteousness.

Let's look at some others that speak forcefully to this group of people. Psalm 41 says:

> All my enemies whisper together against me; they imagine the worst for me, saying, "A vile disease has beset him; he will never get up from the place where he lies." Even my close friend, whom I trusted, he who shared my bread, has lifted up his heel against me. But you, O Lord, have mercy on me; raise me up, that I may repay them (vv. 7-10).

Now consider the expressions of Psalm 109 regarding the one who returned accusations for friendship, repaying evil for good:

Appoint an evil man to oppose him; let an accuser stand at his right hand. When he is tried, let him be found guilty, and may his prayers condemn him. May his days be few; may another take his place of leadership. May his children be fatherless and his wife a widow. May his children be wandering beggars; may they be driven from their ruined homes. May a creditor seize all he has; may strangers plunder the fruits of his labor. May no one extend kindness to him or take pity on his fatherless children. May his descendants be cut off, their names blotted out from the next generation. May the iniquity of his fathers be remembered before the Lord; may the sin of his mother never be blotted out. May their sins always remain before the Lord, that he may cut off the memory of them from the earth (vv. 6-15).

Do we who are pastors preach these psalms? I hope by now you are convinced that we should, and in preaching them show their modern applications and sobering ramifications.

Just as these passages are applied in the New Testament to Judas as the arch-traitor of our Lord, they apply to the false disciples in congregations today who need to hear these frightening imprecations from the pulpit. Such preaching will be healthy for all who hear, so let us take up the gauntlet to preach the whole counsel of God fearlessly.

### Faithful Warriors Need Encouragement

The psalmist constantly prays for the evil of the wicked to come back upon them as their just reward. I call this the "boomerang effect of evil." Listen to his description:

He who is pregnant with evil and conceives trouble gives birth to disillusionment. He who digs a hole and scoops it out falls into the pit he has made. The trouble he causes recoils on himself; his violence comes down on his own head (Ps. 7:14-16).

The psalmist expresses devout thankfulness for these righteous judgments of God! You will find this same spirit in the book of the Revelation of Jesus Christ. The great apostle John relates:

Then I heard the angel in charge of the waters say: "You are just in these judgments, you who are and who were, the Holy One, because you have so judged; for they have shed the blood of your saints and prophets, and you have given them blood to drink as they deserve" (16:5-6).

And echoing again in the Psalms the same thought:

He loved to pronounce a curse—may it come on him; he found no pleasure in blessing—may it be far from him. He wore cursing as his garment; it entered into his body like water, into his bones like oil. May it be like a cloak wrapped about him, like a belt tied forever around him (Ps. 109:17-19).

What men give others comes back to them. We see this principle operating around us daily. Parents who abuse and curse their children often feel the boomerang's blow as the children turn with vicious curses on them. Students who are taught that there is no absolute standard for right and wrong vandalize their own school because they "feel like it." Governments that take advantage of the helpless and needy are ruthlessly destroyed by the exploited masses that rise up in revolution. The gallows that men build to hang others is often used to break their own necks. This is *not* mere chance but God's way of administering justice.

It is *right* to pray for God's righteous judgment, and Christian leaders must teach God's people to pray *in* Christ for the vindication *of* Christ and His church. Unfold these psalms of imprecation with careful obedience, cautioning your listeners against all personal vengeance and anger.

By praying, we put justice in the hands of the righteous Judge of all the earth. The psalmist puts the two together beautifully as he exhorts us after enumerating the treacheries of the wicked: "Cast your cares on the Lord and he will sustain you; he will never let the righteous fall" (Ps. 55:22).

We must remove anger and revenge from our own hands and hearts and commit ourselves to God's wise charge. We please God by evidencing the gentle and peaceable spirit He has given by loving our enemies in Christ. And God *will* hear our prayer in Jesus' name. He *can* be trusted to bring perfect justice in His own time. We have the privilege of teaching God's people to trust the God who will not be mocked.

## Two Present-Day Illustrations

### Chester Bitterman, a Christian Martyr

In February of 1981 I received the shocking news that my friend Chester Bitterman had been kidnapped in Bogota, Colombia. Less than a year previously we had been laboring together in the gospel there.

As a missionary with Wycliffe Bible Translators he had been given an assignment of administrative duty in Bogota and while there had diligently sought out a Spanish-speaking body of believers with whom to worship. In the providence of God I was serving as pastor of that flock at the time, and my family and I came to know and love "Chepe" and his dear family.

One of my family's last evenings in the beautiful city of Bogota was spent in prayer and sweet fellowship with Chepe and his wife as our children played together. Chepe also was an immense help to us in the practical aspects of transporting our possessions as we packed to return to the United States. We had anticipated maintaining a correspondence and being reunited at some later date.

Upon learning of his capture, we prayed incessantly for his release and well-being. He was held captive for forty-eight days. Then word reached us that the terrorists had put a bullet through his heart.

My family and I wept in intense grief. We cried out in Christ for the conversion of these evil people, but also for God's justice to be done. We relinquished to the Lord our very natural feelings of personal hatred and wishes to "get even." Our Lord would bring justice. This is the way we express obedience to our Lord who instructs us, as His disciples, not to repay anyone evil for evil.

In this way we, as leaders, must resolve—and by life and word, instruct God's people—not to take revenge but to leave room for God's wrath. God *has* said, "It is mine to avenge; I will repay" (Rom. 12:19; Deut. 32:35; Heb. 10:30). Yes, by our practice and by our preaching we pass on the orders of our Commander. We teach, and we accompany our congregations, so that together we learn to cry out in our distress as did the Lord's Anointed:

> O Lord, the God who avenges, O God who avenges, shine forth. Rise up, O Judge of the earth; pay back to the proud what they deserve. How long will the wicked, O Lord, how long will the wicked be jubilant? They pour out arrogant words; all the evildoers are full of boasting. They crush your people, O Lord; they oppress your inheritance. They slay the widow and the alien; they murder the fatherless. They say, "The Lord does not see; the God of Jacob pays no heed" (Ps. 94:1-7; see also Ps. 79:10).

We join the psalmist in the confident declaration:

> The Lord has become my fortress, and my God the rock in whom I take refuge. He will repay them for their sins and destroy them for their wickedness; the Lord our God will destroy them (Ps. 94:22-23).

How awesome it is to remember that we are also joined in prayer even now by the company of those already in heaven. Remember what the apostle John saw "under the altar"? It was "the souls of those who had been slain because of the word of God and the testimony they had maintained" (Rev. 6:9). And what were they doing?

> They called out in a loud voice, "How long, Sovereign Lord, holy and true, until you judge the inhabitants of the earth and avenge our blood?" (v. 10).

Do these prayers and affirmations, then, preclude God's bringing salvation to the wicked? Not at all! We must look back and reflect that all Christians, whether in heaven or still on earth, were once among the wicked and rebellious. Remember that Paul, "still breathing out murdering threats" was subdued by sovereign grace (Acts 9). And, praise be to God, He was merciful to us!

So we must always pray that He will have mercy on whom He will have mercy. When will their prayers and ours be answered? Revelation 6:11 answers this urgent question—How long? "They were told to wait a little longer, until the number of their fellow servants and brothers who were to be killed as they had been was completed."

It is our duty now to forgive and love by seeking the repentance and conversion of evildoers. God will act in His own time, and we must forsake all sinful bursts of anger and self-vindication as we bring to Him these cries for justice in the name of the Prince of Peace.

What a comfort it is to *know* that Chepe Bitterman's blood *will* be vindicated—*not by his family or friends but by God Himself!* We pray for the conversion of the men who captured and martyred him, but if they do not repent, we are assured that God's wrath will consume them. We will join the great multitude around the throne shouting:

> Hallelujah! Salvation and glory and power belong to our God, for true and just are his judgments. . . . He has avenged . . . the blood of his servants (Rev. 19:1-2).

If you are in a position of Christian leadership, you have an obligation to teach these precious psalms to God's people as cries for justice that *will be heard!* They are practical and down-to-earth prayers in harmony with Paul's warning:

> God gave them a spirit of stupor, eyes so that they could not see and ears so that they could not hear, to this very day (Rom. 11:8).

He then joins with David in his prayer:

> May their table become a snare and a trap, a stumbling block and a retribution for them. May their eyes be darkened so they cannot see, and their backs be bent forever (Rom. 11:9-10).

Now, you may be saying, "The case with Chester Bitterman is unique. How many times do we experience the death of a martyr of the Lord Jesus Christ?" And I would reply that we must bring to God's people among whom we minister an awareness of the suffering of Christians all over the globe. According to recent statistics, there have been *many millions* of martyrs for Christ *in this century!* Did you know that? With the worldwide communications available today we can become informed and in turn tell brothers and sisters here of the tribulations of the church in a worldwide scope. In this way we join hands and hearts in seeking God's face for those suffering injustices.

## David Rottenberg, a Victim of Crime

I would also like to remind you that these prayers have application not only to Christian martyrs but also to victims who daily suffer loss in our own society through crimes and injustices. At times even we Christians become so accustomed to hearing about crimes that we almost accept them as something we can do nothing to change. But we should be actively involved in making a difference.

When we read the morning newspaper and learn of a drunken driver killing a family through his overindulgence, instead of feeling frustrated and helpless we should allow these psalms to direct us to action. When a case of child abuse is reported on the evening newscast, these prayers of the psalmist lead us to a godly response.

I personally have been very deeply touched by the extreme sufferings and disfigurement of David Rottenberg, a victim of a horrendous crime. On March 3, 1983, he was a beautiful and carefree six-year-old spending a few days in California with his father. He went to sleep in the motel room that night, eagerly anticipating a trip to Disneyland the next day. But while he slept, his father doused the room with three gallons of kerosene, lit a match, and ran. The room literally exploded into flames. Reports said that David's screams could be heard as his father sped away in a car.

The ambulance rushed David to the burn unit of the University of California Irvine Medical Center. Doctors there estimated that he would not survive more than twenty-four hours. Over 90 percent of his little body had suffered severe burns. Horrible pictures of his face and body shocked America as the wires carried the story. How could a father do such a thing? And how are we, as twentieth-century Christians, to respond? With personal hatred and violence? *No!*

We must pray that God will cause this man to be brought to trial and punished for his crime. And through this, we pray also that he will be converted—brought to repentance, to experience God's forgiveness.

The father was arrested and imprisoned. Yet no prison on earth will bring just retribution like God's wrath if he does not repent. This response is not a personal vendetta, but a godly desire to see justice done on earth. Already we can see beauty that has come out of these ashes. Many Christians prayed and some even put feet to their prayers by carrying the good news of salvation into the hospital room to point David and his mother, Marie, to Jesus Christ as Lord and Savior.

If we faithfully expound the whole counsel of God, we are urging His people to pray for justice as they come to terms with very real hurts and injustices in this world. Those who are alienated, lonely, falsely accused, persecuted, and under Satanic attack require the comfort of these prayers. The church must be reminded that her prayers in Christ for justice will be heard, because our God is righteous.

In praying these psalms we identify with those who mourn, those who hunger, those who are exiled, and those who are poor and needy, just as Christ did. Is it not painfully clear as we listen to the preaching of the evangelical church today that it is no longer obedient to the war cries of its Commander? We must resolve with humility to teach God's army how to solicit His aid with the words and spirit of the psalms of justice.

I pray that God will grant powerful preaching from the Psalms of David in order that the prayer life of His church might be renewed. Dietrich Bonhoeffer, the Christian martyr, wrote:

> The Psalter impregnated the life of early Christianity. . . . Whenever the Psalter is abandoned, an incomparable treasure vanishes from the Christian Church. With its recovery will come unsuspected power.[6]

To this we say, "Amen." Let us be faithful messengers of the whole communique from God to His forces here below. And let us pray that He may be pleased to empower His church to overcome evil and extend His everlasting kingdom.

## Questions for Thought and Discussion

1. How do the Psalms reflect God's covenant promises of blessing and cursing?

2. How will Christ fulfill the cries of vengeance of the Psalms?

3. How can the preaching of the imprecatory psalms assist in reminding the church that it is engaged in a serious spiritual warfare?

4. Can you think of any present-day experiences that would illustrate the practical use of these psalms?

5. What is the correlation between the imprecatory psalms and the book of Revelation?

*Notes*

1. Geerhardus Vos, *Biblical Theology* (Grand Rapids: Eerdmans, 1968), p. 100.

2. I recommend E. Calvin Beisner's book *Psalms of Promise—Exploring the Majesty and Faithfulness of God* (Colorado Springs: NavPress, 1988), especially "Curses on Covenant-Breakers," pp. 161-82; vol. 4 of *Search the Scriptures* by C. Vanderwaal (St. Catherines, Ont.: Paideia Press, 1978), especially "Psalms of Imprecation," pp. 49-53; and, from *The Book of Books*, ed. John White (Phillipsburg, N.J.: Presbyterian and Reformed, 1978), the article by Dr. Clarke Copeland, "The Covenant, The Key to Understanding the Bible."

3. *The Cottage Bible and Family Expositor* (Philadelphia: J. W. Bradley, 1849), 1:266.

4. Edmund Clowney, "Preaching Christ From the Psalms," sermon on audio cassette distributed by Westminster Media, Box 27009, Philadelphia, PA 19118.

5. Norval Geldenhuys, *Commentary on the Gospel of Luke* (Grand Rapids: Eerdmans, 1983), p. 475.

6. Dietrich Bonhoeffer, *Psalms: The Prayer Book of the Bible* (Minneapolis: Augsburg, 1970), p. 26.

It is at all times a part of the task of the people of God to destroy evil. Once we see this we do not, for instance, meanly apologize for the imprecatory Psalms but glory in them.

Cornelius Van Til
*Christian Theistic Ethics*

# 7

# Marching to War
# in God's Kingdom!

## The Glory of All the Saints

Many are asking today, "Where has all the glory gone?" They look at the explosive growth of the early church and read of the courageous exploits of Christian heroes through the centuries and are understandably disillusioned by today's church. Has this present lack of vigor resulted, at least in part, from failure to attack the kingdom of darkness by forceful prayer and preaching? What does God tell us about the source of our glory as His saints?

> Let the saints rejoice in this honor and sing for joy on their beds. May the praise of God be in their mouths and a double-edged sword in their hands, to inflict vengeance on the nations and punishment on the peoples, to bind their kings with fetters, their nobles with shackles of iron, to carry out the sentence written against them. This is the glory of all his saints. Praise the Lord (Ps. 149:5-9).

How does this psalm instruct the saints to experience the glory? First, by executing vengeance on the nations; second, by binding the kings of the nations with chains; and third, by carrying out the sentence written against them. It is painfully clear from this passage that those who reject the imprecatory prayers have lost their ordained glory and strength.

*The Weapons of Our Warfare*

God plainly declares that it is His purpose to bring down the evil empire in due time. But how has He chosen to do so? Through the prayers and work of His saints—your prayers and mine! We must end the wishy-washy, milquetoast prayers of our own philosophies and learn again to beg for the overthrow of Satan's domain.

Satan has gained an advantage by stopping the powerful prayers of the saints against his kingdom for entirely too long! The church has thought itself too good and too mature for these war cries of justice. In doing so it has unwittingly fallen for Satan's strategy. This has proven to be a costly error.

We must now urgently pray and preach these psalms for the destruction of evil in the earth. This is our heritage. The apostles and the early church prayed and preached this way. The Reformers of every century have battled valiantly for the realization of God's kingdom, and they have been world-changing forces in their time. *Now the banner of truth has been handed to us.* Will we let it fall? God's kingdom is still at war!

How should you fight this kingdom warfare? Not with the carnal weapons of this world, but rather "in truthful speech and in the power of God; with weapons of righteousness in the right hand and in the left" (2 Cor. 6:7).

Christianity conquered the world in the early centuries, but it was not the physical conquest of battles between peoples. There followed a sad period in history when for nearly two hundred years (1095–1291) in a series of Crusades ("Holy Wars") thousands of people were slaughtered in the name of Christianity. In more modern times as well, vast numbers of professing Christians have drawn their weapons from carnal arsenals, but followers of the living and true God are *not* called to engage in that "holy war." The horror and sinfulness of the Crusades should serve as a warning that our weapons are not physical. Paul's words continue to echo down to us:

> The weapons we fight with are not the weapons of the world. On the contrary, they have divine power to demolish strongholds (2 Cor. 10:4).

*Prayer and preaching are the powerful weapons that overcome the world!* We pray for the destruction of the evil empire, and through these prayers God brings down the very gates of hell in the name of Jesus Christ. Where do we learn to pray like this? From these very prayers that have been cast off as "out-of-date," "devilish," and "inferior"—the imprecatory psalms. That's why we must faithfully preach from these psalms and pray them in the Lord Jesus Christ.

### The Conflict of the Ages

The conflict we perceive in the Psalms is the great conflict of the ages. This is the ultimate warfare of life. Jack Scott reminds us of its fundamental nature with these words:

> The enemy is first God's enemy. The enmity is set by God. The enemy is hostile because of his sin and the believer puts his trust in God to deliver him from the enemy. The enemy is an oppressor and persecutor, and the psalmist anticipates ultimate triumph over the enemy as God has shown in past history. To identify the enemy on a personal basis is to ignore all that has preceded. Clearly the psalmist is looking at history and recognizing that God has made a distinction. God has put enmity between those who trust in God and those who do not (the children of God and the children of Satan). This makes believers and unbelievers enemies, not on the basis of personal likes and dislikes, but on the basis of the two kingdoms (of God and of the world). The psalmist's enemies are God's enemies (Ps. 5:4, 5; 139:22, 23).[1]

Have we lost sight of the fact that we are at war with the enemies of God? Have we been guilty of playing at Christianity in our comfortable churches, exchanging "warm fuzzies" and pleasant chit-chat? If so, it is time to wake up!

If it was warfare for Christ's church in the first century, it is warfare today. If it was war in the sixteenth century, then it is war in the twentieth century. Soldiers of Christ, arise!

*Our Present Task*

*Prayer*

Listen to the words of Calvin Beisner:

> Prayer is, in fact, spiritual warfare. One weapon is prayer for
> conversion of spiritual enemies; another is prayer for judgment
> on those who finally refuse to be converted. We handicap the
> army of God when we refuse to use both of these great weapons
> that He has given us.[2]

Jay Adams drew my attention to an illustration offered by
Spurgeon in his *Treasury of David*, which I think puts a proper
perspective on our prayers:

> I cannot forbear the following little incident that occurred the
> other morning at family worship. I happened to be reading one
> of the imprecatory psalms, and as I paused to remark, my little
> boy, a lad of ten years, asked with some earnestness: "Father, do
> you think it right for a good man to pray for the destruction of
> his enemies like that?" and at the same time referred me to Christ
> as praying for his enemies. I paused a moment to know how to
> shape the reply so as to fully meet and satisfy his enquiry, and
> then said, "My son, if an assassin should enter the house by night,
> and murder your mother, and then escape, and the sheriff and
> citizens were all out in pursuit, trying to catch him, would you
> not pray to God that they might succeed and arrest him, and that
> he might be brought to justice?" "Oh, yes!" said he, "but I never
> saw it so before. I did not know that that was the meaning of these
> psalms." "Yes," said I, "my son, the men against whom David
> prays were bloody men, men of falsehood and crime, enemies to
> the peace of society, seeking his own life, and unless they were
> arrested and their wicked devices defeated, many innocent per-
> sons must suffer." The explanation perfectly satisfied his mind.[3]

What a glorious privilege is ours to pray for the capture and
punishment of Satan and all his followers!

*Proclamation With Praise*

As we pray for His kingdom to come, we are to use the Word of God as the sword that will demolish evil by the faithful proclamation of His truth. The faithful Christian and apologist Cornelius Van Til calls us to our duty with these words:

> It is at all times a part of the task of the people of God to destroy evil. Once we see this we do not, for instance, meanly apologize for the imprecatory psalms but glory in them.[4]

Part of that glorying in them involves proclaiming them in song. We have put great emphasis in this work on the Psalms as the "prayer book" of the church. In conclusion I'd like to remind you that it's also the only "song book" God has included in His Word. Its prayers and praises were designed to be *sung!*

Now, the normal pattern for us is to *say* many things, but when we burst into *song*, that is usually an indication of heartfelt *joy*. Let's not stop short of the goal of teaching the people of God under our care to sing these psalms with hearts full of love for the Lord who bought us. In this way, we'll be preparing them to sing that "new song" before the throne of the Lamb throughout eternity (Rev. 5:1-12). And finally we will shout:

> Hallelujah! Salvation and glory and power belong to our God, for true and just are his judgments. He has condemned the great prostitute who corrupted the earth by her adulteries. He has avenged on her the blood of his servants. . . . Hallelujah! (Rev. 19:1-3).

If you have been guilty of dulling your sword, the one part of your armor that is an offensive weapon, by neglecting or undermining these psalms, repent of that sin, sharpen your sword anew, and go forth to do battle in the name and for the glory of King Jesus—that the knowledge of the Lord will cover the earth as the waters cover the seas (Hab. 2:14). "Let them know that you, whose name is the Lord—that you alone are the Most High over all the earth" (Ps. 83:18).

Amen.

*Questions for Thought and Discussion*

1. What pitfalls must we guard against in seeking to restore the imprecatory psalms in the life of Christ's church?

2. Review how we are to use the psalms of vengeance and the dangers of their misuse or neglect.

3. Consider how all the Psalms may be sung in your congregation.

4. How can the praying of these psalms in Christ lead to reformation and revival in your local church?

**Notes**

1. In John H. Skilton, ed., *The Law and the Prophets* (Phillipsburg, N.J.: Presbyterian and Reformed, 1974), p. 134.

2. E. Calvin Beisner, *Psalms of Promise* (Colorado Springs: NavPress, 1988), p. 180.

3. Charles H. Spurgeon, *The Treasury of David* (London: Passmore and Alabaster, 1882), p. 170.

4. Cornelius Van Til, *Christian Theistic Ethics* (Nutley, N.J.: Presbyterian and Reformed, 1980), p. 84.

# Appendix 1

# "The Christian's Duty Towards His Enemies"

## by Robert L. Dabney

*Robert Dabney (1820-98), one of the great theologians of the nineteenth century in America, taught systematic theology for many years. He also served as Chaplain and then as Chief of Staff to Stonewall Jackson during the Civil War. Archibald Alexander of Princeton said that Dabney was "the best teacher of theology in the United States if not the world." The following is an excerpt from "The Christian's Duty Towards His Enemies." Dabney's full address can be found in* Discussions: Evangelical and Theological, *vol. 1 (London: Banner of Truth, 1967).*

It may be surmised that this is a duty whose "metes and bounds" are ill understood by many of the people of God, and that, consequently, the minds of many of them are harassed with doubts and temptations concerning it. On the one hand, many, perhaps, excuse to themselves criminal emotions under the name of virtuous indignation, and on the other some of them afflict themselves with compunctions for and vain endeavors against feelings which are both proper and natural to us as rational beings.

The embarrassment is increased by the current opinion that there is inconsistency between the teachings and examples of the Old Testament and the New upon this subject. Men read in the former the stern language of the imprecatory Psalms, for instance, of the thirty-fifth, the thirty-ninth,[1] the one hundred and ninth, the one hundred and thirty-seventh, and the one hundred and thirty-ninth, where the inspired man prays: "Let them be confounded and put to shame that seek after my soul. . . . Let them be as chaff before the wind, and let the angel of the Lord chase them"; or describes the persecuted church as crying to her oppressors: "Happy shall he be that rewardeth thee as thou hast served us"; or protests: "Do not I hate them, O Lord, that hate thee? And am I not grieved with those that rise up against thee? I hate them with perfect hatred." They then turn to the Sermon on the Mount and read the words of our Lord: "But I say unto you, Love your enemies, bless them that curse you, do good to them that hate you, and pray for them which despitefully use you and persecute you." They thereupon imagine a discrepancy, if not a contradiction, between them, and adopt the mischievous conclusion that the two Testaments contains different codes of Christian ethics. This notion, it is to be feared, has a general prevalency. What is more common than to hear Christians, who should be well informed, and who profess full reverence for the inspiration of the whole Scriptures, speak of the morality of the Old Testament, of the Hebrew saint, of the prophet, as harsh, austere, and forbidding, while that of the New Testament, of Jesus, and of the Christian is sweet and forgiving?

All these notions are of Socinian or rationalistic origin, and are incompatible with an honest belief in the actual inspiration of the Scriptures. If inspiration is but an "elevation of the consciousness," a quickening of the intuitions of the transcendental reason, an exaltation of the soul, of the same generic kind with the other impulses of genius, only of a higher grade, then it can be understood how prophets and apostles may contradict each other; although yet they may teach us noble lessons, and such as common men would never have found out of themselves. But if "all Scripture (the apostle means the Old Testament) is theopneustic," if "holy men of old spake as they were moved by the Holy Ghost," and the apostles, in their turn, had the promise of the Holy Ghost to "lead them into all truth," then a real discrepancy between them is impossible; for all truths must be harmonious among themselves. The honest believer can admit, of course, that the partial revelation of the Old Testament, although absolute truth as far as it goes, and as perfect in its principles as the God who gave it, stops short of that fulness of detail to which the New Testament afterwards proceeded. But while there is a difference in degrees of fulness, there can be no contrariety.

The same view commends itself irresistibly to the plain mind from this fact, that Jesus Christ, not to add the apostles, suspended the truth of his mission and doctrines on the infallibility and holiness of the Old Testament. His appeal is ever to them. He cites Moses and the prophets as though he thought their testimony must be the end of strife. Now, if they are not inspired and true, it follows irresistibly that Jesus Christ was either mistaken or he was dishonest. *Absit impietas.* In either case, he is no Redeemer for us. And, indeed, the former alternative of this dilemma is inadmissible for one who claimed, as he did, an infallible knowledge for himself, a preexistence of the era of Abraham and the prophets and the authority of the Messiah by whose Spirit those prophets spoke. So that, if the Old Testament were imperfect, Jesus of Nazareth would stand convicted of criminal attempts of imposture!

There is a second reason why such an explanation cannot be applied to the supposed vindictiveness of Old Testament morals: that the same sentiments are expressed in the New Testament, and the same maxims of forbearance which are cited as so lovely in the latter are set forth, both by precept and example, in the former; so that, if a discrepancy is asserted, it must not be between David and Christ, Hebrew and Christian, but both Testaments must be charged with contradicting themselves, as well as each other. Thus, in Acts viii. 20, Peter exclaims to Simon Magus, "Thy money perish with thee!" In Acts xxiii. 3, Paul sternly denounces the persecuting chief priest, "God shall smite thee, thou whited wall!" and in 2 Tim. iv. 14 distinctly expresses a prayer for retribution upon Alexander, the coppersmith of Ephesus: He "did me much evil; the Lord reward him according to his works." In 2 Thess. i. 7-10, Christ's coming "in flaming fire to take vengeance

on them that know not God," is subject of admiration in all them
that believe. In the Apocalypse vi. 10, the souls of the martyrs
under the altar are heard crying with a loud voice: "How long, O
Lord, holy and true, dost thou not judge and avenge our blood
on them that dwell on the earth?" And in Matt. xi. 20, and xxiii.
13, Jesus of Nazareth is heard denouncing awful woes upon the
enemies of truth.

On the other hand, the Old Testament contains substantially
the same precepts of forgiveness, and example of forbearance,
which are so much admired in the New. First, the great truth,
which lies at the root of all this subject, that retribution is the
exclusive function of the Lord, was first published in the Old
Testament, and it is thence Paul quotes it, in Rom. xii. 10,[2] "It is
written, Vengeance is mine, saith the Lord." It is written a thou-
sand years before (Deut. xxxii. 35; Lev. xix. 18), "To me belongeth
vengeance and recompense"; recognized by David as a rule for
him (1 Sam. xxiv. 12) towards his deadly enemy, Saul,—"the Lord
judge between me and thee, and the Lord avenge me of thee; but
my hand shall not be upon thee"; repeated in Psalm xciv. 1, "O
Lord God, to whom vengeance belongeth"; and cited against evil
men, as a rule which they had violated, twice in Ezek. xxv. 12, 15,
"Edom and the Philistines have taken vengeance, and have greatly
offended." The lovely precept for rendering good for evil is
enjoined upon the Israelites in a form most perspicuous and
impressive to a pastoral people: "If thou meet thine enemy's ass
or his ox going astray, thou shalt surely bring it back to him
again." (Exod. xxiii. 4.) Israel was enjoined to practice tenderness
towards foreigners, a duty ignored then by the pagan world, and
especially toward Egyptians, their late ruthless oppressors.
(Exod. xxii. 21; Deut. xxiii. 7.) Job, the oldest of the patriarchs
whose creed has been handed down to us, recognizes malice,
even when limited to the secret wishes, as an iniquity: "If I re-
joiced at the destruction of him that hated me, or lifted up myself
when evil found him; neither have I suffered my mouth to sin by
wishing a curse to his soul." (Job xxxi. 29.) David, the author of
nearly all the imprecatory Psalms, repudiates malice with holy
abhorrence: "If I have rewarded evil to him that was at peace with

me; (yea, I have delivered him that without cause is mine enemy,) let the enemy persecute my soul and take it," etc. (Ps. vii. 4.) And in Psalm xxxv. 13, he describes his deportment towards his enemies, as in contrast with theirs towards him, and in strict accordance with Christ's command: "But as for me, when they were sick, my clothing was sackcloth; I humbled my soul with fasting," etc. That all this was not mere profession, we have splendid evidence in the sacred history, where he displayed such astonishing forbearance and magnanimity towards Saul, after the most vehement provocation; twice delivering his life from the indignation of his followers, and singing his dirge with the honorable affection of a loyal follower.

This age has witnessed a whole spawn of religionists, very rife and rampant in some sections of the church, who pretentiously declared themselves the apostles of a lovelier Christianity than that of the sweet Psalmist of Israel. His ethics were entirely too vindictive and barbarous for them, forsooth; and they, with their Peace Societies, and new lights, would teach the world a milder and more beneficent code! How impertinent does this folly appear, coming from the petted favorites of fortune, whose wilfulness and conceit had hitherto been pampered by a rare concurrence of privileges, so that they had hardly experienced the call for the Christian virtue of forgiveness; and who, as soon as they are crossed (not in their rights, but) in their most arrogant caprices, show themselves incapable of one throb of David's magnanimity, and break out into a vindictiveness set on fire of hell! He who knows his own heart and human nature will humbly avow, instead of accusing the Psalms of unchristian malice, that he will do well if he never goes beyond their temper, under bitter wrong, and if, while swelling with righteous sense of injury, he can always remit the retribution, in wish, as in act, to God alone.

The consequence of this erroneous admission of actual discrepancy between the morality of the Old Testament and the New is, that expositors have fatigued themselves with many vain inventions to explain away the imprecatory language of the Psalms. The generality of this feeling is betrayed by the frequency of these attempts. A curious betrayal of this skeptical impression exists to this day, in the book of Psalms, in the hands of our own Presbyterian people. Instead of a metrical version of Psalm cix., as it stands in the inspired lyrics, there is a human composition upon the beauty of forgiveness. In the psalm books in use for a whole age among the Presbyterians of England and this country, this hymn was formerly prefaced with the words (Psalm cix.), "Christian forgiveness after the example of Christ." This title the last editors of our psalm book bethought themselves to omit. Anyone who compared the human poem with the actual hundred and ninth Psalm could hardly fail to overlook the suggestion of a contrast, that while the uninspired psalmist of our modern Israel gave utterance to Christian forgiveness after the example of Christ, the actual ode of inspiration expressed unchristian revenge after the example of David. How could the feeling be more clearly betrayed that the sentiments of the psalmist were indefensible?[3]

Hence ingenious expedients have been sought to explain them away. Of these, the most current is the following: that where our version says, for instance, "Let his days be few, and let another take his office," the verbs are improperly rendered as imperatives. It is asserted that they may as fairly be rendered as simple future, "His days will be few," etc., and then all these passages are converted from imprecations to predictions. The psalmist only foretells the divine retributions. Waiving the insuperable difficulty, that it is only to a part of these texts the explanation even plausibly applies, we perceive this general objection: that if they be all understood as predictions only, yet they are predictions to the accomplishment of which the inspired men evidently looked forward with moral satisfaction. Thus they reveal precisely the same sentiments towards evildoers as though we understood them as appealing to God with requests for their righteous retribution, while they at the same time recognize his sole title to avenge, and the sinfulness of their taking their retaliation into their own hands.

All these inventions, then, must be relinquished; the admission must be squarely and honestly made, that the inspired men of both Testaments felt and expressed moral indignation against wrong-doers, and a desire for their proper retribution at the hand of God. This admission must also be successfully defended, which, it is believed, can be done in perfect consistency with that spirit of merciful forbearance and love for the persons of enemies which both Testaments alike inculcate.

*Notes*

1. Printing error. It should read the "sixty-ninth," instead of the thirty-ninth.

2. Reference should read Romans 12:19.

3. See also *Rejoice in the Lord*, ed. Erik Routley (Grand Rapids: Eerdmans, 1985), Psalm 137 "By the Babylonian Rivers." Stanza 4 removed the inspired word for "another" (Hymnal of Reformed Church in America).

# Appendix 2

# Two Sermon Summaries

## *"CONDEMNATION, VENGEANCE, AND REJOICING"*

Psalm 58:

Do you rulers indeed speak justly? Do you judge uprightly among men? No, in your heart you devise injustice, and your hands mete out violence on the earth. Even from birth the wicked go astray; from the womb they are wayward and speak lies. Their venom is like the venom of a snake, like that of a cobra that has stopped its ears, that will not heed the tune of the charmer, however skillful the enchanter may be.

Break the teeth in their mouths, O God; tear out, O Lord, the fangs of the lions! Let them vanish like water that flows away; when they draw the bow, let their arrows be blunted. Like a slug melting away as it moves along, like a stillborn child, may they not see the sun.

Before your pots can feel the heat of the thorns—whether they be green or dry—the wicked will be swept away. The righteous will be glad when they are avenged, when they bathe their feet in the blood of the wicked. Then men will say, "Surely the righteous still are rewarded; surely there is a God who judges the earth."

On July 11, 1937, Dietrich Bonhoeffer, who was later martyred for his stand against Hitler and the Third Reich, preached from this psalm. His sermon was not a theoretical exercise by an armchair theologian. It was a bold war cry in the midst of increasing persecution of the confessing church. The Nazi Gestapo arrested 804 members of the confessing church during that year. In fact, just a few days before preaching from this text Bonhoeffer himself had spent a day under arrest. Confiscations, interrogations, house searches, and arrests charged the atmosphere with fear and unrest as the young minister began his sermon. Listen carefully to his well-chosen words:

> Is this fearful psalm of vengeance to be our prayer? May we pray in this way? Certainly not! We bear much guilt of our own for the action of any enemies who cause us suffering. We must confess the righteous punishment of God in that which afflicts and humbles us sinful human beings. Even in these times of distress for the church, we must confess that God himself has raised his hand in wrath against us, in order to visit our sins upon us: our spiritual indolence, our open or hidden disobedience, our great lack of discipline in daily living under his Word. Or would we deny that every personal sin, even the most hidden one, must bring down God's wrath upon his congregation? How then should we, who are guilty ourselves and deserving of God's wrath call down God's vengeance upon our enemies? Will not this vengeance much more strike us? No, we cannot pray this psalm. Not because we are too good for it (what a superficial idea, what colossal pride!), but because *we are too sinful, too evil for it!*[1]

How then can we ever make this psalm our prayer? Can we learn to sing this psalm with God's people of old? What's involved in this psalm?

> *First*, the accusation of the wicked.
> *Second*, the prayer for the destruction of evil.
> *Third*, the rejoicing in God's judgment.

## I. How Can You Accuse the Wicked?

### A. Who Is Doing the Accusing in This Psalm?

Only one who is just can rightfully accuse others of injustice; only someone who is guiltless can pray this way. This psalm is the prayer of the innocent man. According to its title, David is the author of this psalm. So David prays this psalm; but *he* is not innocent. How then could he pray it? We need to remember that he was the Lord's anointed in the Old Testament, the forerunner of Christ. God was bringing through David the One who would be called David's greater Son—Jesus Christ. For that reason David must not perish at the hand of his enemy. David could never have prayed against his enemies this way on his own behalf or merely to preserve his own life. David's practice, as you recall, was to endure meekly all the personal abuse hurled at him. But Christ was in David, so David's enemies are the enemies of Jesus Christ. Truly the innocent Christ was praying this psalm with David. God Himself is here accusing the wicked of their guilt.

## B. What Are the Accusations?

1. (v. 1) Leaders are silent when the helpless are persecuted and exploited. When you hear others crying for help and turn a deaf ear, Christ stands up to accuse you of sin. Millions of unborn babies are put to death in America while the judges of this world keep silent. No, worse than that, they actually justify (in their own minds, at least) the killing of the unborn as an exercise of American liberty. They speak a biased word against justice. They call good what God calls evil. David himself was silent about his sins against Uriah until the accusing word of Christ came to him through the prophet Nathan—"You are the man!"

2. (v. 2) Not only do this world's rulers fail to oppose injustices, but their hearts and hands are busy with violence and oppression. Pilate examined Jesus and found Him innocent, but that did not ensure Jesus' release, did it? Instead, Pilate gave the order to crucify Him!

3. (v. 3) Corrupt ways are the result of a sinful nature. The infection of a sinful nature extends even to each unborn human embryo. Satan has hold on his own even in the womb. Psalm 51:5 says: "Surely I have been a sinner from birth; sinful from the time my mother conceived me." And Psalm 58:3: "Even from birth the wicked go astray; from the womb they are wayward and speak lies."

Notice that with this verse a change is made. Instead of being addressed, the tyrants are now described. But we must recognize that the difference between these evildoers and David himself is one of degree rather than of kind. He too was a sinner from the womb. And the description in verses 3-5 resembles Romans 3:10-18 so closely that each of us is reminded that we are not looking at a portrait but a mirror!

4. (vv. 4-5) No one will independently leave Satan's control. Only God's grace can convert you. These next verses tell of the stubborn persistence of the wicked in their sinful ways. They refuse to hear God's gracious call. They have "stopped [their] ears." Neither the most loving persuasion nor the most powerful preaching can change their minds. They "will not heed the tune of the charmer, however skillful the enchanter may be." If we have been granted repentance unto life while others have not yet, we cannot boast as though it were our own work, but humbly give thanks to God who has made the difference.

The wicked are determined covenant breakers. Only He that is without sin can hurl these powerful accusations.


## II. How Can You Pray for the Destruction of Evil Rulers?

Verses 6-8 contain a strongly worded prayer for vengeance on the wicked. It is important that we proceed with caution here so that we do not sin in our prayer.


### A. How Not to Pray

These cries for vengeance were not a personal vendetta of David's, as we can see from Psalm 35:12-14:

> They repay me evil for good and leave my soul forlorn. Yet when they were ill, I put on sackcloth and humbled myself with fasting. When my prayers returned to me unanswered, I went about mourning as though for my friend or brother. I bowed my head in grief as though weeping for my mother.

Some Christians have abused such a prayer by using it against anyone who would oppose them personally. Preachers from coast to coast are urging their congregations to pray for the utter destruction of anyone who questions their authority or lifestyle. One pastor even said, "We're tired of turning the other cheek.... Good heavens, that's all that we have done." This is *not* the spirit of the psalm. We must not pray these fierce petitions upon our personal enemies. We have rather been called to show Christ's love and forgiveness to our enemies, renouncing all personal vengeance. Only in Jesus Christ can we ever pray these frightful cries for God's justice to be made known in the earth.

### B. Lessons for Prayer

1. God will bring justice to the wicked. He will avenge the blood of His righteous ones. It is His right as Creator to execute vengeance. "It is mine to avenge; I will repay," God says in Deuteronomy 32:35 and again in Romans 12:19. And Paul warns us in Galatians 6:7: "Do not be deceived: God cannot be mocked. A man reaps what he sows."

2. God is setting up His kingdom and He will ultimately destroy the kingdom of Satan and all its subjects. He alone knows who those subjects are and when and how they are to be destroyed. We must wait His time and pray fervently as our Lord taught us, "Your kingdom come, your will be done on earth as it is in heaven."

3. Our prayers should reflect these truths. Like the psalmist we should pray for the disarmament and the utter annihilation of any who will not bow the knee to Christ: "God, now step in and destroy *your* enemy. Use your power, let your righteous wrath blaze forth" (Bonhoeffer). God will bring just judgment upon His enemies, and its execution will be fierce. The prayers of the psalmist will be fulfilled in all their force. The mighty hand of God will crush all the wicked for the sake of His supreme kingdom, name, and honor.

### III. How Can You Rejoice When God Judges the World? (vv. 9–11)

### A. Rejoice—God's Judgment Is Righteous!

You can only rejoice in God's final judgment if you are in Christ. Otherwise you will be among those destined for destruction as covenant breakers.

## B. Rejoice—God's Judgment Is Necessary!

We shudder at this psalm, but if we reject it we are rejecting God and His holiness. The psalm says that "the righteous will be glad" (v. 10) (statement of fact)! Do you find this hard to accept? Bonhoeffer didn't mince matters when he said, "Whoever shrinks from this joy in the vengeance of God and in the blood of the wicked does not yet know what took place on the cross of Christ." Only as God's wrath is poured out on the sinner can we see justice in the earth. But we find deliverance from the judgment of God against us only in Jesus Christ who bore God's wrath in our place at Golgotha. He became a curse for us that we might be redeemed (Gal. 3:13-14). Bonhoeffer says it so well:

> Whoever comes to him, whoever cleaves to him, will never more be touched by the wrath and vengeance of God. That person is in the protection of the righteousness of Christ, whoever he may be. Whoever will not come, whoever will not cast himself down before the cross of Christ, whoever despises the cross, will suffer God's wrathful judgment, the vengeance of God, as it came upon Christ—but not unto life, rather unto eternal death.

## C. Rejoice—God's Judgment Is Sure!

He will bring justice to the earth. In Revelation the apostle records what he saw at the final time:

> The angel swung his sickle on the earth, gathered its grapes and threw them into the great winepress of God's wrath. They were trampled in the winepress outside the city, and blood flowed out of the press, rising as high as the horses' bridles for a distance of 1,600 stadia (14:19-20).

And again, "I saw heaven standing open and there before me was a white horse, whose rider is called Faithful and True. With justice he judges and makes war" (Rev. 19:11). Our psalm says, "*Surely* the righteous still are rewarded; *surely* there is a God who judges the earth" (v. 11).

God calls us to action. The psalmist's words become Christ's very own. As our sinless representative He accuses the wicked, calls down God's vengeance, and rejoices in the reward of those who are righteous through His blood. In the words of Bonhoeffer:

> And now we, too, pray this psalm with Him, in humble thanks that we have been granted deliverance from wrath through the cross of Christ; in the fervent plea that God will bring all of our (mutual) enemies under the cross of Christ and grant them grace; in the burning desire that the day may soon come in which Christ visibly triumphs over His enemies and establishes His kingdom.

There will be justice on the earth as God delivers the righteous and damns the wicked. This powerful psalm speaks as much to our own day as to Bonhoeffer's. May we thus learn to pray this psalm in Christ.

> The victories of that Just One, gained in his own person, and in those of his faithful servants, over the enemies of man's salvation, are productive of a joy, which springeth not from love of revenge, but is inspired by a view of the Divine mercy, justice, and truth, displayed in the redemption of the elect, the punishment of the ungodly, and the accomplishment of the promises. Whoever duly weigheth and considereth these things, will diligently seek after the reward of righteousness, and humbly adore the Providence which ordereth all things aright in heaven and earth.
>
> George Horne

> The enemies of God are implacable. It is necessary for the vindication of God's authority and God's goodness that just retribution should not be long delayed. He prays for it, not shutting his eyes to the horrors which it involves. There is no sadistic pleasure in seeing his enemy suffer, no sense of getting his own back, but simply a deep desire that the world might see that God is just.
>
> John Wenham

## *"CHRIST'S FINAL VICTORY"*

Psalm 137:8-9:

> O Daughter of Babylon, doomed to destruction,
> happy is he who repays you
> for what you have done to us—
> he who seizes your infants
> and dashes them against the rocks.

This passage of Holy Scripture has been attacked as fiercely as any words in all the Bible. One modern commentator says, "The ironic 'bitter beatitudes' of verses 8 and 9, the very reverse of true religion, are among the most repellent words in Scripture."[2]

This is just one of multitudes of such comments. The widespread misinterpretation of these verses has caused many to react with feelings of repulsion toward this psalm. It has been misrepresented as filled with malice, vengeance, and delight in the sufferings of others. Probably the most horrendous perversion of this psalm has been circulated by the liberation theologians, whose version of Psalm 137 appeared in one of their books in Spanish. Compare the following blatant distortion with what God gave in His Word:

> Captives of the gringos
> we cried with bitterness
> while seeing from behind jail bars
> the sky scrapers of Babel-York,
> when we remembered you, Latin America.
> From the roof hung the silent guitars
> and our captors relieve their boredom
> by asking us, "Sing us a song from your land."
> How can we sing the sweet songs
> of Latin America while in
> a strange country?
> If I forget you, marvelous Latin America,
> may my hands shrivel like dried herbs
> and my tongue stick to the roof of my mouth
> if I lose your memory.
> May sharks devour my corpse
> if I don't hold the liberation

of your borders
before my own life and goods.
Remember, O Father of History,
to punish the gringo assassin
on the day of liberation
of our land.
Take in consideration the actions
of those beasts thirsty
for the lifeblood of our country,
when they mockingly said,
"Let us be done with the ugly Latin,
may none remain on the earth!"
O gringo democracy, filthy prostitute,
happy is the one who succeeds
in returning to you hundredfold
all the evil you have done!
Happy is he who dashes you
like chicks against the ground,
all the CIA agents
and all the bloody generals of the Pentagon.[3]

You can see how liberation theologians have twisted God's Word to make it serve their own purpose. And this is just one of many distortions of these important verses.

What is the *correct* understanding of this psalm?

We will focus our attention on the last two verses of this psalm, but in arriving at them we see the setting of the people of Judah in captivity. Their sorrow and grief are intense, and the nostalgia for their homeland overwhelms them. As the psalmist reflects on the many cruelties they had endured, he begins to pray and ask God to bring justice to the wicked. And so we come to our text, verses 8-9, which have been so misunderstood and frequently rejected even by Christians.

Before we see how these verses are to be properly understood and how they apply to us today, there is some necessary background information from the text and the original language. The final and most offensive words of our text—"dashes your infants against the rocks"—are the only words from this entire psalm chosen for repetition in the New Testament. And in what context or setting do we find them? Our Lord Jesus Christ speaks them in Luke 19:44. The verb that we have translated here as "dashes" from the Greek occurs only twice in Scripture: first in the Septuagint version of our verse (Ps. 137:9) and then in its New Testament citation in the lament of our Lord over Jerusalem. The reserving of this particular verb for this specific use in all of Scripture shows how our Lord deliberately referred to this psalm. Isaiah prophesied (13:16) the Lord's wrath upon Babylon, whose "infants will be dashed to pieces," and in Psalm 137:8-9 we hear the psalmist yearning for the Lord to fulfill His prophecy. Our Lord in Luke 19:41-44 prophesied similar judgment upon the city that rejects the Lord's Anointed One. We need a New Testament understanding of our passage. When we see it in that light, it will be transformed from sentences of doom and malice to words of triumph and encouragement.

## I. Christ Will Triumph Over His Enemies

We begin by defining some terms.

### A. Who Is the "Daughter of Babylon" Who Is "doomed to destruction"?

She represents all that is hostile to God. The climax of the history of Babylon is her destruction as pronounced in Revelation 18:2: "Fallen! Fallen is Babylon the Great!" This cry for her destruction is an echo of God's promise in Jeremiah 51:56—"A destroyer will come against Babylon; her warriors will be captured, and their bows will be broken. For the Lord is a God of retribution; he will repay in full"—and in Isaiah 13—"An oracle concerning Babylon . . . 'Their infants will be dashed to pieces before their eyes; their houses will be looted and their wives ravished. . . . Babylon, the jewel of kingdoms, the glory of the Babylonians' pride, will be overthrown by God like Sodom and Gomorrah" (vv. 1, 16, 19). (See also Isa. 21:1-10, 47; Jer. 50-51; Hab. 2:4-20.)

## B. Who Are the "infants" Destined to Be "dashed"?

The Hebrew word here means "children" and does not specify the *age* but the *relationship*. All those who are followers of the evil kingdom (children of Babylon) will be dashed to pieces (Ps. 2:9; Jer. 19:11; Rev. 12:5; 19:15). (*'Ollel* in Hebrew and *nepios* and *teknon* in Greek do not specify the *age* but the *relationship*.)

## C. Are Christ's Enemies Your Enemies?

They were certainly the psalmist's sworn enemies. He so closely identified with his God that it was natural for him to loathe intensely those set against God. He speaks under inspiration of the Holy Spirit, *not harboring a personal grudge or expressing a personal vindictiveness against his own enemies.* It is true that wicked men hate God, and their hatred is an evil emotion. The psalmist's hatred is like God's hatred, reflecting a supreme desire that the purposes of God's kingdom will flourish and wickedness be destroyed.

In Psalm 139:19-22 we find the spirit of the psalmist clearly given:

> If only you would slay the wicked, O God! Away from me, you bloodthirsty men! They speak of you with evil intent; your adversaries misuse your name. Do I not hate those who hate you, O Lord, and abhor those who rise up against you? I have nothing but hatred for them; I count them my enemies.

Then he prays, "Search me, O God, and know my heart; test me and know my anxious thoughts. See if there is any offensive way in me, and lead me in the way everlasting" (vv. 23-24). Here is perfect hatred expressed against the enemies of God. It is the hatred each of us should have to properly honor our holy God. You need to ask yourself right now, "Are Christ's enemies my enemies?" If they are not, you do not love the Lord as you should!

## II. Christ Will Destroy His Enemies With the "rock"

### A. What Is the "rock" That Will Bring Destruction?

This is surely metaphorical language and not literal since Babylon is built on a flat alluvial plain without cliffs or rocks.

No intelligent dweller in Babylonia, heathen or servant of Jehovah, could fail to understand the metaphor of Babylon's being hurled from her exaltation in pride and power, for the literal interpretation is ridiculous, no cliffs or rocks or mountains being anywhere near.[4]

The Hebrew text has the word "rock" in the singular, not plural, as is reflected by the ASV, 1901. Notice the correlation to Jesus' words in Matthew 21:42-44, as he teaches concerning the future:

Have you never read in the Scriptures: "The stone the builders rejected has become the capstone; the Lord has done this, and it is marvelous in our eyes"? Therefore I tell you that the kingdom of God will be taken away from you and given to a people who will produce its fruit. He who falls on this stone will be broken to pieces, but he on whom it falls will be crushed. (See also Dan. 2:34-35.)

This is the same word for "rock" used in Numbers 20:8ff. (See also Ps. 114:8.) This is the "rock" from which the apostle Paul said the forefathers drank, and he tells the Corinthians plainly, "that rock was Christ" (1 Cor. 10:4).

### B. Why Will This Happen?

The "Daughter of Babylon" and her "infants" have rejected Christ, the Rock. The curses that will come upon Babylon the Great will be a returning to her of the torture and grief she has given others. Jeremiah recorded the cry of God's people so long ago and God's promise:

"May the violence done to our flesh be upon Babylon," say the inhabitants of Zion. "May our blood be on those who live in Babylonia," says Jerusalem. Therefore, this is what the Lord says: "See, I will defend your cause and avenge you; I will dry up her sea and make her springs dry" (Jer. 51:35-36).

And the apostle John heard a voice from heaven say of Babylon the Great:

her sins are piled up to heaven, and God has remembered her crimes. Give back to her as she has given; pay her back double for what she has done. Mix her a double portion from her own cup. Give her as much torture and grief as the glory and luxury she gave herself. In her heart she boasts, "I sit as queen; I am not a widow, and I will never mourn." Therefore in one day her plagues will overtake her: death, mourning and famine. She will be consumed by fire, for mighty is the Lord God who judges her (Rev. 18:5-8).

Let all who are enemies of God read their doom in the ashes of Babylon.

### III. Christ's Final Victory Will Involve You!

#### A. Will You Be Among Those Destroyed?

There are curses pronounced upon all who forsake the Lord. Psalm 137:5-6 pronounces God's curse upon anyone who forgets Jerusalem and the Lord that gave meaning to the Holy City. Even the psalmist himself is not exempt from the curse: "May my tongue cling to the roof of my mouth if I do not remember you." All who depart from the Lord are part of Babylon. There are only two kingdoms in the world: the kingdom of Satan ("Babylon the Great") and the kingdom of Christ. And Christ's kingdom will surely dash to pieces Babylon and all the kingdom of darkness. It is essential that you determine of which kingdom you are a part. If you are in the kingdom of Satan today, your doom is sure. Unless you become part of the kingdom of Christ, you will be among those destroyed in Christ's final victory.

#### B. Will You Be Among Those Rejoicing?

When Christ's victory is finally realized, there will be great rejoicing. John gives us another peek into the heavenly scene in Revelation 18-19:

"Rejoice over her, O heaven! Rejoice, saints and apostles and prophets! God has judged her for the way she treated you." . . . In her was found the blood of prophets and of the saints, and of all who have been killed on the earth. After this I heard what sounded like the roar of a great multitude in heaven shouting, "Hallelujah! Salvation and glory and power belong to our God, for true and just are his judgments. He has condemned the great prostitute who corrupted the earth by her adulteries. He has avenged on her the blood of his servants." And again they shouted: "Hallelujah! The smoke from her goes up for ever and ever." The twenty-four elders and the four living creatures fell down and worshipped God, who was seated on the throne. And they cried: "Amen, Hallelujah!" Then a voice came from the throne, saying: "Praise our God, all you his servants, you who fear him, both small and great!" Then I heard what sounded like a great multitude, like the roar of rushing waters and like loud peals of thunder, shouting: "Hallelujah! For our Lord God Almighty reigns. Let us rejoice and be glad and give him glory!" (18:20, 24; 19:1-7a).

Our psalm assures us: "Happy is he who repays you" (v. 8). This rejoicing will exceed all the gladness of the world. Joyful "Hallelujahs" will be sung by all God's people on that day. I pray that you will be among them!

*For further study: For historical background I refer you to the outstanding article of Howard Osgood, "Dashing the Little Ones Against the Rock,"* Princeton Theological Review *1(1903):23-37. Also see* Walter C. Kaiser, Jr., Hard Sayings of the Old Testament *(Downers Grove: InterVarsity, 1988), pp. 171-75.*

Notes

1. Quotations from Bonhoeffer were taken from his sermon "A Psalm of Vengeance—Psalm 58," in Dietrich Bonhoeffer, *Meditating on the Word* (Cambridge, Mass.: Cowley Publications, 1986).

2. R. E. O. White, *A Christian Handbook to the Psalms* (Grand Rapids: Eerdmans, 1984), p. 200.

3. Angel Gonzalez, *El Libro de los Salmos—Introduccion, version y comentario* (Barcelona: Herder, 1966), a free translation by James and Nancy Adams.

4. Howard Osgood, "Dashing the Little Ones Against the Rock," *Princeton Theological Review* 1(1903):35.

# Appendix 3

# Index to Psalm Imprecations

The spirit of the imprecations of the Psalms is found throughout the Psalter. The psalmist desires the destruction, shame, judgment, fear, silence, defeat, scattering, persecution, confusion, and death of his enemies in many of the psalms. The following verses are only the formal cries to God for His judgment upon the wicked.

These formal imprecations call for God to blot out, desolate, and utterly destroy the wicked; but many other psalms that are not listed here as containing formal imprecation express the same desire. For instance, Psalm 21 is not found in the list, but it speaks with joy of God's wrath upon the wicked:

> Your hand will lay hold on all your enemies; your right hand will seize your foes. At the time of your appearing you will make them like a fiery furnace. In his wrath the Lord will swallow them up, and his fire will consume them. You will destroy their descendants from the earth, their posterity from mankind (vv. 8-10).

It should be noted that all of these cries for justice commit the problem to the Lord and leave vengeance to God. They show faith toward God in the context of real-life situations and at the same time express a holy moral indignation against all who would set themselves against God's King and kingdom. This is the spirit of the Psalms from beginning to end.

| | | | |
|---|---|---|---|
| 5:10 | 55:15 | 74:23 | 109:11 |
| 6:10 | 56:7 | 79:6 | 109:12 |
| 7:6 | 58:6 | 79:10 | 109:13 |
| 9:19 | 58:7 | 79:11 | 109:14 |
| 9:20 | 58:8 | 79:12 | 109:15 |
| 10:2 | 58:9 | 83:9 | 109:16 |
| 10:15 | 58:10 | 83:10 | 109:17 |
| 17:13 | 59:5 | 83:11 | 109:18 |
| 25:19 | 59:11 | 83:12 | 109:19 |
| 28:4 | 59:12 | 83:13 | 109:29 |
| 31:17 | 59:13 | 83:14 | 119:84 |
| 31:18 | 59:14 | 83:15 | 129:5 |
| 35:1 | 63:9 | 83:16 | 129:6 |
| 35:4 | 63:10 | 83:17 | 129:7 |
| 35:5 | 68:1 | 83:18 | 137:7 |
| 35:6 | 68:2 | 94:1 | 137:8 |
| 35:8 | 68:30 | 94:2 | 137:9 |
| 35:19 | 69:22 | 94:3 | 139:19 |
| 35:24 | 69:23 | 94:4 | 139:21 |
| 35:25 | 69:24 | 97:7 | 139:22 |
| 35:26 | 69:25 | 104:35 | 140:8 |
| 40:14 | 69:27 | 109:6 | 140:9 |
| 40:15 | 69:28 | 109:7 | 140:10 |
| 41:10 | 70:2 | 109:8 | 140:11 |
| 54:5 | 70:3 | 109:9 | 141:10 |
| 55:9 | 71:13 | 109:10 | 143:12 |

# Appendix 4

# New Testament References to the Psalms

This list contains direct quotations, allusions, and fulfillments of the Psalms in the New Testament. This is not an exhaustive list but is helpful for interpreting the Psalms. (List prepared by Jonathan E. Adams.)

| Psalm | New Testament Reference | Psalm | New Testament Reference |
|---|---|---|---|
| 1:2 | Rom. 7:22 | 7:13 | Eph. 6:16 |
| 2:1 | Rev. 11:18 | 8:3 (LXX) | Matt. 21:16 |
| 2:1-2 | Acts 4:25-26 | 8:5-7 (LXX) | Heb. 2:6-8 |
| 2:7 | Matt. 3:17; 17:5 | 8:6 | 1 Cor. 15:27 |
| | Mark 1:11; 9:7 | | Eph. 1:22 |
| | Luke 3:22; 9:35 | 9:2 | Rev. 19:7 |
| | John 1:49 | 9:4 | 1 Pet. 2:23 |
| | Acts 13:33 | 9:8 | Acts 17:31 |
| | Heb. 1:5; 5:5 | 9:20 | Luke 21:26 |
| 2:8 | Heb. 1:2 | 10:7 | Rom. 3:14 |
| 2:8, 9 | Rev. 2:26-27 | 10:16 | Rev. 11:15 |
| 2:9 | Rev. 12:5; 19:15 | 11:6 | Rev. 14:10; 20:10 |
| 2:11 | Phil. 2:12 | | Rev. 21:8 |
| 4:4 | Eph. 4:26 | 14:1-3 | Rom. 3:10-12 |
| 5:9 | Rom. 3:13 | 14:7 | Rom. 11:26-27 |
| 6:3 | John 12:27 | 16:8-11 | Acts 2:25-28 |
| 6:8 | Matt. 7:23 | 16:9 | John 20:9 |
| | Luke 13:27 | 16:10 | Acts 2:31 |
| 7:9 | Rev. 2:23 | | 1 Cor. 15:4 |
| 7:12 | Luke 13:3, 5 | 16:10 (LXX) | Acts 13:35 |

| Psalm | New Testament Reference | Psalm | New Testament Reference |
|---|---|---|---|
| 17:15 | Rev. 22:4 | 29:3 | Acts 7:2 |
| 18:2 | Luke 1:69 | 31:5 | Luke 23:46 |
| 18:4 | Acts 2:24 | | Acts 7:59 |
| 18:6 | James 5:4 | | 1 Pet. 4:19 |
| 18:49 | Rom. 15:9 | 31:24 | 1 Cor. 16:13 |
| 19:1 | Rom. 1:20 | 32:1-2 | Rom. 4:7-8 |
| 19:4 | Rom. 10:18 | 32:2 | Rev. 14:5 |
| 19:9 | Rev. 16:7; 19:2 | 32:5 | 1 John 1:9 |
| 21:9 | James 5:3 | 33:2-3 | Eph. 5:19 |
| 22:1-31 | 1 Pet. 1:11 | 33:3 | Rev. 5:9; 14:3 |
| 22:1 | Matt. 27:46 | 33:6, 9 | Heb. 11:3 |
| | Mark 15:34 | 34:8 | Heb. 1:14 |
| 22:1-18 | Mark 9:12 | | 1 Pet. 2:3 |
| | Luke 24:27 | 34:12-16 | 1 Pet. 3:10-12 |
| 22:5 | Rom. 5:5 | 34:13 | James 1:26 |
| 22:7 | Matt. 27:39 | 34:14 | Heb. 12:14 |
| | Mark 15:29 | 34:15 | John 9:31 |
| 22:7-8 | Luke 23:35-36 | 34:19 | 2 Cor. 1:5 |
| 22:7, 8 | Matt. 26:24; 27:43 | | 2 Tim. 3:11 |
| 22:15 | John 19:28 | 34:20 | John 19:36 |
| 22:16 | Phil. 3:2 | 35:8 | Rom. 11:9-10 |
| 22:16-18 | Matt. 26:24; 27:35 | | 1 Thess. 5:3 |
| | Mark 15:24 | 35:11 | Matt. 26:60 |
| | Luke 23:34 | 35:13 | Rom. 12:15 |
| | John 19:24 | 35:16 | Mark 10:34 |
| 22:20 | Phil. 3:2 | | Acts 7:54 |
| 22:21 | 2 Tim. 4:17 | 35:19 | John 15:25 |
| 22:22 | Heb. 2:12 | 36:1 | Rom. 3:18 |
| 22:23 | Rev. 19:5 | 36:9 | Rev. 21:6 |
| 22:28 | Rev. 11:5; 19:6 | 37:4 | Matt. 6:33 |
| 23:1 | John 10:11 | 37:11 | Matt. 5:5 |
| | Rev. 7:17 | 37:12 | Acts 7:54 |
| 23:2 | Rev. 7:17 | 38:11 | Luke 23:49 |
| 23:5 | Luke 7:46 | 39:1 | James 1:26 |
| 24:1 | 1 Cor. 10:26 | 39:12 | Heb. 11:13 |
| 24:3-4 | Matt. 5:8 | | 1 Pet. 2:11 |
| 25:11 | 1 John 2:12 | 40:3 | Rev. 5:9; 14:3 |
| 25:20 | Rom. 5:5 | 40:6 | Eph. 5:2 |
| 25:21 | Luke 6:27 | | Heb. 10:8 |
| 26:6 | Matt. 27:24 | 40:6-8 | Heb. 10:5-7 |
| 26:8 | Matt. 23:21 | 40:8 | Matt. 26:39 |
| 28:4 | Matt. 16:27 | 41:9 | Matt. 26:23 |
| | 2 Tim. 4:14 | | Mark 14:18 |
| | 1 Pet. 1:17 | | Luke 22:21 |
| | Rev. 20:12-13; 22:12 | | |

| Psalm | New Testament Reference | Psalm | New Testament Reference |
|---|---|---|---|
| | John 13:18; 17:12 | | Rev. 20:12-13 |
| | Acts 1:16 | | Rev. 22:12 |
| 41:13 | Luke 1:68 | 65:7 | Luke 21:25 |
| | Rom. 9:5 | 66:10 | 1 Pet. 1:7 |
| 42:2 | Rev. 22:4 | 66:18 | John 9:31 |
| 42:5,11 | Matt. 26:38 | 67:2 | Acts 28:28 |
| | Mark 14:34 | 67:36 (LXX) | 2 Thess. 1:10 |
| | John 12:27 | 68:8 | Heb. 12:26 |
| 43:5 | Matt. 26:38 | 68:18 | Eph. 4:8 |
| | Mark 14:34 | 68:26 | Heb. 2:12 |
| 44:22 | Rom. 8:36 | 69:4 | John 15:25 |
| 45:6-7 | Heb. 1:8-9 | 69:8 | John 7:5 |
| 46:2-3 | Luke 21:25 | 69:9 | John 2:17 |
| 46:6 | Rev. 11:18 | | Rom. 15:3 |
| 47:8 | Rev. 4:2, 9, 10 | 69:13 | 2 Cor. 6:2 |
| | Rev. 5:1, 7, 13 | 69:14-16 | Heb. 5:7 |
| | Rev. 6:16; 7:10, 15 | 69:15 | Acts 2:24 |
| | Rev. 19:4; 21:5 | 69:21 | Matt. 27:34, 48 |
| 48:2 | Matt. 5:35 | | Mark 15:23, 36 |
| 50:6 | Heb. 12:23 | | Luke 23:36 |
| 50:12 | Acts 17:25 | | John 19:29 |
| | 1 Cor. 10:26 | 69:22 | 1 Thess. 5:3 |
| 50:14 | Heb. 13:15 | 69:22-23 | Rom. 11:9-10 |
| 50:16-21 | Rom. 2:21 | 69:23 | 2 Cor. 3:14 |
| 50:23 | Heb. 13:15 | 69:24 | Rev. 16:1 |
| 51:1 | Luke 18:13 | 69:25 | Matt. 23:38 |
| 51:4 | Luke 15:18 | | Luke 13:35 |
| | Rom. 3:4 | | Acts 1:20 |
| 51:5 | John 9:34 | 69:28 | Phil. 4:3 |
| | Rom. 7:14 | | Rev. 3:5; 13:8 |
| 53:1-3 | Rom. 3:10-12 | | Rev. 17:8; 20:12 |
| 55:14 | Acts 1:16, 17 | | Rev. 20:15; 21:27 |
| 55:15 | 1 Thess. 5:3 | 72:10-11 | Rev. 21:26 |
| 55:22 | 1 Pet. 5:7 | 72:10, 11 | Matt. 2:11 |
| 58:10 | Rev. 19:3 | 72:15 | Matt. 2:11 |
| 59:3 | Mark 3:2 | 72:18 | Luke 1:68 |
| | Luke 6:7 | 74:2 | Acts 20:28 |
| 59:4 | Matt. 5:11 | 75:8 | Rev. 14:10; 15:7 |
| 62:10 | Matt. 19:22 | | Rev. 16:19 |
| | 1 Tim. 6:17 | 78:2 | Matt. 13:35 |
| 62:12 | Matt. 16:27 | 78:4 | Eph. 6:4 |
| | Rom. 2:6 | 78:8 | Acts 2:40 |
| | 2 Tim. 4:14 | 78:15 | 1 Cor. 10:4 |
| | 1 Pet. 1:17 | 78:24 | John 6:31 |
| | Rev. 2:23 | | Rev. 2:17 |

| Psalm | New Testament Reference | Psalm | New Testament Reference |
|---|---|---|---|
| 78:24-29 | 1 Cor. 10:3 | 97:1 | Rev. 19:6 |
| 78:31 | 1 Cor. 10:5 | 97:3 | Rev. 11:5 |
| 78:37 | Acts 8:21 | 97:7 | Heb. 1:6 |
| 78:44 | Rev. 16:4 | 98:1 | Rev. 5:9; 14:3 |
| 79:1 | Luke 21:24 | 98:3 | Luke 1:54 |
| | Rev. 11:2 | | Acts 28:28 |
| 79:3 | Rev. 16:6 | 98:9 | Acts 17:31 |
| 79:5, 6 | Rev. 6:9-10 | 99:1 | Rev. 19:6 |
| 79:6 | 1 Thess. 4:5 | 102:4, 11 | James 1:10-11 |
| | 2 Thess. 1:8 | 102:25-27 | Heb. 1:10-12 |
| | Rev. 16:1 | 103:3 | Mark 2:7 |
| 79:10, 11 | Luke 18:7 | 103:7 | Rom. 3:2 |
| | Rev. 6:10; 19:2 | 103:8 | James 5:11 |
| 82:6 | John 10:34 | 103:13, 17 | Luke 1:50 |
| 86:9 | Rev. 15:4 | 104:2 | 1 Tim. 6:16 |
| 88:8 | Luke 23:49 | 104:4 | Heb. 1:7 |
| 88:8 (LXX) | 2 Thess. 1:10 | 104:12 | Matt. 13:32 |
| 89:3-4 | John 7:42 | 105:8-9 | Luke 1:72-73 |
| 89:4 | John 12:34 | 105:21 | Acts 7:10 |
| 89:10 | Luke 1:51 | 105:40 | John 6:31 |
| 89:11 | 1 Cor. 10:26 | 106:10 | Luke 1:71 |
| 89:20 | Acts 13:22 | 106:14 | 1 Cor. 10:6 |
| 89:26 | 1 Pet. 1:17 | 106:20 | Rom. 1:23 |
| 89:27 | Rev. 1:5 | 106:25-27 | 1 Cor. 10:10 |
| 89:36 | John 12:34 | 106:37 | 1 Cor. 10:20 |
| 89:50-51 | 1 Pet. 4:14 | 106:45-46 | Luke 1:72 |
| 90:4 | 2 Pet. 3:8 | 106:48 | Luke 1:68 |
| 91:11 | Luke 4:10 | 107:3 | Matt. 8:11 |
| | Heb. 1:14 | | Luke 13:29 |
| 91:11-12 | Matt. 4:6 | 107:9 | Luke 1:53 |
| 91:12 | Luke 4:11 | 107:20 | Acts 10:36 |
| 91:13 | Luke 10:19 | 109:3 | John 15:25 |
| 92:5 | Rev. 15:3 | 109:4, 5, 7, 8 | John 17:12 |
| 93:1 | Rev. 19:6 | 109:8 | Acts 1:20 |
| 94:1 | 1 Thess. 4:6 | 109:20 | 2 Tim. 4:14 |
| 94:11 | 1 Cor. 3:20 | 109:25 | Matt. 27:39 |
| 94:14 | Rom. 11:1, 2 | | Mark 15:29 |
| 94:19 | 2 Cor. 1:5 | 109:28 | 1 Cor. 4:12 |
| 95:7-8 | Heb. 3:15; 4:7 | 110:1 | Matt. 22:44; 26:64 |
| 95:7-11 | Heb. 3:7-11 | | Mark 12:36; 14:62 |
| 95:11 | Heb. 3:18; 4:3; 4:5 | | Mark 16:19 |
| 96:1 | Rev. 5:9; 14:3 | | Luke 20:42-43 |
| 96:11 | Rev. 18:20 | | Luke 22:69 |
| 96:13 | Acts 17:31 | | Acts 2:34-35 |
| | Rev. 19:11 | | Rom. 8:34 |

| Psalm | New Testament Reference | Psalm | New Testament Reference |
|---|---|---|---|
| | 1 Cor. 15:25 | 122:1-5 | John 4:20 |
| | Eph. 1:20 | 125:5 | Gal. 6:16 |
| | Col. 3:1 | 125:5-6 | Luke 6:21 |
| | Heb. 1:3, 13; 8:1 | 128:6 | Gal. 6:16 |
| | Heb. 10:12, 13; 12:2 | 130:8 | Titus 2:14 |
| 110:4 | John 12:34 | | Rev. 1:5 |
| | Heb. 5:6, 10; 6:20 | 132:1-5 | Acts 7:45-46 |
| | Heb. 7:3, 17, 21 | 132:11 | Acts 2:30 |
| 111:2 | Rev. 15:3 | 134:1 | Rev. 19:5 |
| 111:4 | James 5:11 | 135:1 | Rev. 19:5 |
| 111:9 | Luke 1:49, 68 | 135:14 | Heb. 10:30 |
| 112:9 | 2 Cor. 9:9 | 135:15-17 | Rev. 9:20 |
| 112:10 | Acts 7:54 | 137:8 | Rev. 18 |
| 113-118 | Matt. 26:30 | 137:9 | Matt. 21:43, 44 |
| 114:3-7 | Rev. 20:11 | | Luke 19:44; 20:18 |
| 115:4-7 | Rev. 9:20 | 139:1 | Rom. 8:27 |
| 115:13 | Rev. 11:18; 19:5 | 139:14 | Rev. 15:3 |
| 116:3 | Acts 2:24 | 139:21 | Rev. 2:6 |
| 116:10 | 2 Cor. 4:13 | 140:3 | Rom. 3:13 |
| 116:11 | Rom. 3:4 | | James 3:8 |
| 117:1 | Rom. 15:11 | 141:2 | Rev. 5:8; 8:3, 4 |
| 118:6 | Rom. 8:31 | 141:3 | James 1:26 |
| | Heb. 13:6 | 143:2 | Rom. 3:20 |
| 118:18 | 2 Cor. 6:9 | | 1 Cor. 4:4 |
| 118:20 | John 10:9 | | Gal. 2:16 |
| 118:22 | Luke 20:17 | 144:9 | Rev. 5:9; 14:3 |
| | Acts 4:11 | 145:17 | Rev. 15:3; 16:5 |
| | 1 Pet. 2:4, 7 | 145:18 | Acts 17:27 |
| 118:22-23 | Matt. 21:42 | 146:6 | Acts 4:24; 14:15 |
| | Mark 12:10-11 | | Acts 17:24 |
| 118:25-26 | Mark 11:9 | | Rev. 10:6; 14:7 |
| | John 12:13 | 147:8 | Acts 14:17 |
| 118:26 | Matt. 21:9; 23:39 | 147:9 | Luke 12:24 |
| | Luke 13:35; 19:38 | 147:18 | Acts 10:36 |
| 119:46 | Rom. 1:16 | 147:19-20 | Rom. 3:2 |
| 119:137 | Rev. 16:5, 7; 19:2 | 149:1 | Rev. 5:9; 14:3 |
| 119:165 | 1 John 2:10 | | |

# Bibliography

## Help From Good Books

This is a partial list of books I have enjoyed and found helpful on this subject. I have read hundreds of books and articles during my years of research, but I have selected thirty-seven of the best, which I hope will be a help in preaching from the imprecatory psalms.

Augustine. "Expositions on the Book of Psalms." In vol. 8 of *A Select Library of the Nicene and Post-Nicene Fathers of the Christian Church*, Series I. Edited by Philip Schaff. Grand Rapids: Eerdmans, 1983.

Beisner, E. Calvin. *Psalms of Promise: Exploring the Majesty and Faithfulness of God*. Colorado Springs: NavPress, 1988. Note especially "Curses on Covenant-Breakers," pp. 161-82. Excellent material even in footnotes.

Bernardino, Nomeriano C. "A Reconsideration of 'Imprecations' in the Psalms." Th.M. thesis, Calvin Theological Seminary, 1986.

Binnie, William. *The Psalms: Their History, Teachings, and Use*. London: Hodder and Stoughton, 1886. Excellent!

Bonar, Andrew A. *Christ and His Church in the Book of Psalms*. Grand Rapids: Kregel, 1978.

Bonhoeffer, Dietrich. *Life Together*. San Francisco: Harper and Row, 1954. Pages 44-50 are outstanding!

Bonhoeffer, Dietrich. *Psalms: The Prayer Book of the Bible*. Minneapolis: Augsburg, 1970. Worth its weight in gold!

Calvin, John. *Commentary on the Book of Psalms*. Grand Rapids: Baker, 1981. This monumental work demonstrates the careful-

ness with which Calvin investigated the grammatical and literal meaning of the Hebrew text. He affirms the inspiration of
the imprecatory psalms and stresses that they are never to be
used to justify any personal vendetta or hatred of our enemies.
Calvin's strict historical method of interpretation was a reac-
tion against the allegorical spiritualizing of previous expositors. His deficiency consists in his failure to see the messianic
interpretation given by Christ and His apostles to the Psalms.

Clowney, Edmund P. *The Unfolding Mystery: Discovering Christ in
the Old Testament.* Colorado Springs: NavPress, 1988. Superb
biblical theology!

Copeland, Clarke. "The Covenant, the Key to Understanding the
Bible." In *The Book of Books,* edited by John White, pp. 299-337.
Phillipsburg, N.J.: Presbyterian and Reformed, 1978.

Delitzsch, Franz. *Commentary on the Old Testament.* Vol. 5. Grand
Rapids: Eerdmans, n.d. Good survey of the history of the exposition of the Psalms.

Dick, James. "The Imprecatory Psalms." In *Psalm-Singers' Conference,* pp. 87-96, Belfast: Fountain Printing, 1903. Many useful
addresses in this volume on the ethical and christological understanding of the Psalms.

Dickson, David. *A Commentary on the Psalms.* 2 vols. Minneapolis:
Klock and Klock. There is also a Banner of Truth one-volume
edition.

Eaton, J. H. *Psalms Introduction and Commentary.* London: S.C.M.,
1967. Though I do not agree with all of his interpretations, he
has some outstanding material on the messianic kingship of
the Psalms.

Gurnall, William. *The Christian in Complete Armour; A Treatise of
the Saints' War Against the Devil.* Carlisle, Pa.: Banner of Truth,
1974, pp. 444-48.

Hengstenberg, E. W. *The Works of Hengstenberg,* vols. 5-7, *Commentary on the Psalms.* Cherry Hill: Mack, n.d. Hengstenberg holds
the orthodox position that there are no ungodly prayers in the
Psalms as they are all the inspired Word of God. Fine exegetical
material.

Horne, George. *A Commentary on the Book of Psalms.* Philadelphia: Whetham, 1833.

Kaiser, Walter C., Jr. *Hard Sayings of the Old Testament.* Downers Grove, Ill.: InterVarsity, 1988. (Ps. 137:8-9, pp. 171-75.)

Kaiser, Walter C., Jr. *Toward Old Testament Ethics.* Grand Rapids: Zondervan, 1983, pp. 292-97.

Kidner, Derek. *An Introduction and Commentary on Books I and II and III-V of the Psalms.* In *The Tyndale Old Testament Commentaries,* edited by D. J. Wiseman. Downers Grove, Ill.: InterVarsity, 1973 and 1975.

Leupold, H. C. *Exposition of the Psalms.* Grand Rapids: Baker, 1969.

Luther, Martin. *Luther's Works.* Edited by Jaroslav Pelikan. St. Louis: Concordia, n.d. In all of his works on the Psalms Luther preaches Christ from the imprecatory psalms.

Martin, Chalmers. "Imprecations in the Psalms." *Princeton Theological Review* 1 (1903): 537-53. This work was reprinted in *Classical Evangelical Essays in Old Testament Interpretation,* compiled and edited by Walter C. Kaiser, Jr. Grand Rapids: Baker, 1972.

McNaugher, John, ed. *The Psalms in Worship.* Pittsburgh: United Presbyterian Board of Publication, 1907, pp. 297-320.

Mennega, Harry. "The Ethical Problem of the Imprecatory Psalms." Master's thesis, Westminster Theological Seminary, 1959.

Old, Hughes Oliphant. "The Psalms as Christian Prayer, a Preface to the Liturgical Use of the Psalter." Th.D. diss., Calvin College, 1977.

Olsen, Erling C. *Meditations in the Book of Psalms.* New York: Loizeaux Brothers, 1952.

Osgood, Howard. "Dashing the Little Ones Against the Rock," in *Princeton Theological Review* 1 (1903): 23-37. Outstanding study for preaching from Psalm 137.

Poole, Matthew. *A Commentary on the Holy Bible.* Edinburgh: Banner of Truth, 1979. Note especially his comments on Psalm 95.

Prothero, Rowland E. *The Psalms in Human Life.* New York: E. P. Dutton, n.d. Helpful work on the history of how the church has used and abused the Psalms. The scriptural index gives numerous references on each psalm.

Spurgeon, Charles H. *The Treasury of David.* Vol. 1. London: Passmore and Alabaster, 1882. Notice especially quotations of old commentaries. A must for every library.

Vanderwaal, Cornelis. *Search the Scriptures.* Vols. 1. and 4. St. Catherines, Ont.: Paideia Press, 1978.

Vos, Johannes G. "The Ethical Problem of the Imprecatory Psalms." *Westminster Theological Journal* (May, 1942): 123-38. Excellent!

Waltke, Bruce K. "A Canonical Process Approach to the Psalms." In *Tradition and Testament—Essays in Honor of Charles Lee Feinberg,* edited by Paul Feinberg and John Feinberg. Chicago: Moody Press, 1981. Excellent article on the New Testament understanding of the Psalms. Excerpt: "We conclude, then, that the Psalms are ultimately the prayers of Jesus Christ, Son of God. He alone is worthy to pray the ideal vision of a king suffering for righteousness and emerging victorious over the hosts of evil. As the corporate head of the church, he represents the believers in these prayers. Moreover, Christians, as sons of God and as royal priests, can rightly pray these prayers along with their representative Head."

Wenham, John W. *The Goodness of God.* Downers Grove, Ill.: Inter-Varsity, 1974, pp. 148-72.

Young, Edward J. *Psalm 139: A Devotional and Expository Study.* London: Banner of Truth, 1965. Great preaching material!

And last but not least, an excellent volume for singing the Psalms: *The Book of Psalms for Singing,* 7418 Penn Avenue, Pittsburgh, Pennsylvania 15208.